# How does your Birmingham grow?

From the John Whybrow Collection of old and new photographs. Edited by John Whybrow

# Contents

First edition October 1972
ISBN 0 9502459 0 9
Copyright notice © John Whybrow 1972
All rights reserved. No part of this
publication may be reproduced, stored in a
retrieval system, or transmitted, in any form
or by any means, electronic, mechanical,
photocopying, recording or otherwise,
without the prior permission of
John Whybrow Limited.

Endpapers; enlarged section of New Street,
Birmingham, c.1895. See page 60.
The caption for each photograph in this
book is preceded by an 'H' number. This
is the negative number in the
John Whybrow Collection.

Design and illustrations by John Broadhurst

Published by John Whybrow Limited,
200 Stratford Road, Birmingham B11 1AB
England.
Set in 8pt and 10pt Baskerville.
Printed by Burrows and Smith Limited,
Birmingham B11 4PB, England.

# Preface

**The Lord Mayor's Parlour,**
**The Council House,**
**Birmingham, B1 1BB**

'How does your Birmingham grow?'
is really a long-lost family album
belonging to the people of this city.
John Whybrow and his team are
to be congratulated in gathering
the material and publishing the
book in such an attractive and
enjoyable way.

Birmingham is a famous place for
inventing and making things.
Perhaps because of this we are often
too busy to reflect where we have
come from or where we are going.
This book stops us in our tracks.

In particular I commend 'How
does your Birmingham grow?' to
the young people of this city. In a
few fleeting years they will hold the
reigns of government. A knowledge
of our yesterday will help them
with their tormorrow. For older
members of our community I am
sure the photographs will bring
back many happy memories of
when their world too was young.

Alderman F. T. D. Hall
Lord Mayor

# Introduction

by John Whybrow

I was nine years old when my father showed me the old Birmingham glass negatives taken by Thomas Lewis. He gave me a lesson on what to do if you dropped one. The trick was to catch it with your foot.

I saw plenty of broken glass seven years later when Birmingham was bombed in 1940. Windows were shattered and homes were destroyed. Some streets disappeared completely. It dawned on me for the first time that buildings actually had to be constructed, carefully brick by brick, by men working to a plan. I looked again at the old negatives to see how, in fact, Birmingham had grown.

Each of these silent negatives was protected by a piece of plain stiffish buff paper, wrapped round to overlap at the back. There were three negative sizes: 12-inch by ten-inch, 8½-inch by 6½-inch and 6½-inch by 4¾-inch

Early Victorian professional photographers did not have enlargers. It was like the three bears. If a client wanted a big picture you took out the big camera. If he needed a middle-sized photograph you prepared the next one down. And so on. If the client was specific and required a big picture and a baby one this meant two cameras.

When I joined the company, then called Lewis & Randall Limited, I practised making prints from the old negatives. At the same time, in 1947, I began cataloguing them and collecting material about Thomas Lewis. However, I was more concerned with becoming a photographer myself. I had to try to be better than my father before clients would accept me as being even half as good as they thought he was. Young men following in their fathers' footsteps will know all about this feeling. So apart from occasional use the old negatives stayed in their cardboard boxes awaiting our centenary.

Nearly twenty-five years passed. In 1971 a selection of the old views was made and prints from them were given to a member of the staff, Miss Elizabeth Clair Jones. Elizabeth was asked to photograph the changes that had taken place.

To duplicate the original view-points it was often necessary to go into buildings across the street and to photograph from windows or roofs. The old prints proved more effective than a search warrant for gaining admission. Occupiers were fascinated. Furniture was dragged aside and windows which had not been used for years were forced open. Ladders were found to climb onto roofs. Rope was provided to haul up the camera. Whatever had to be done was done. From top management to the cleaners, all felt personally involved in helping Elizabeth to photograph history.

Way back in 1871, when Thomas Lewis was embarking on his career in Birmingham, England, the wide straight streets and avenues of another Birmingham were being marked out. This year I was privileged to visit that city in Alabama, to see what they had achieved and to take some photographs. I hope the negatives, together with Elizabeth Jones' new records of Birmingham, England, will be preserved. Perhaps in A.D. 2072 the double exercise will be repeated and the story of the Birminghams extended. If so, then to future historians, before they are tempted to make comparisons and say how 'interesting' we are, I would point out, more or less firmly, that neither the Americans nor the British are *quaint*. We are right up-to-date.

The Victorians, of course, were just the same *they* had all the latest gadgets, too. So when we study the photographs in this book perhaps we will smile not so much with amusement but rather with kinship and affection.

*Birmingham, July 1972.*

# The Birmingham Story

by Martin Hedges

Watt's Rotative Steam Engine 1788.

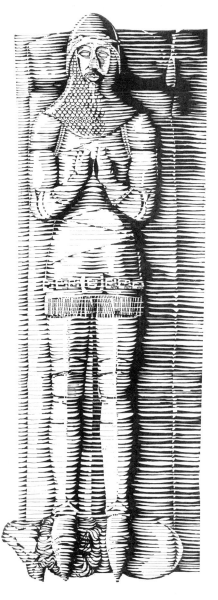

After the Norman Conquest, at which time the people were subject to a Lord named Ulwin, the Manor was given to Richard, who became known as Richard de Bermingham, a vassal of William FitzAnsculf, Lord of Dudley Castle. FitzAnsculf tenants also held the manors of Handsworth, Witton, Erdington, Aston, Edgbaston and Selly Oak.

By 1166 Peter de Bermingham had secured from Henry II the right to hold a market in the village, which meant that he was able to levy tolls. His descendants held the manor for nearly 400 years, though William (one of seven William de Berminghams), who supported Simon de Montfort and the barons against Henry III, was slain at the Battle of Evesham and his estates forfeit.

Honour – and the estates – were restored to his son, the next William, who fought in the French wars and was granted the right to hold a spring fair.

*Effigy of an early de Bermingham in St. Martin's Church, Birmingham.*

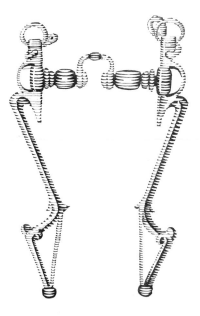

By 1538 John Leland was describing the manor, chapel, smiths and cutlers of Deritend and writing of crossing the bridges over the Rea which were maintained by the Gild of the Holy Cross, and walking 'up the mene hill' into Birmingham itself, where the smithies used to make knives 'and all manner of cuttynge tooles and lorimars that make byts and a great many naylors. So that a great parte of the towne is mayntayned by smithies having yren out of Staffordshire and Warwickshire and see coale out of Staffordshire'. By then, too, there were also tan yards, fulling mills and blade mills in this village which had grown to be a town.

*Mediaeval horse bit.*

Birmingham's original attractions as a settling place were almost certainly the site's pleasant southern slope above a convenient watering place, the River Rea, at a point where it was crossed by the Roman Ryknield Street. The first settlers were probably Saxons, who, led by their chieftain, Beorma, could well have made their way along Ryknield Street or along the River Tame to reach the area in the 6th century.

Apart from the Rea itself, they would have found good waterside meadows, stretches of heath for pasturing their herds and flocks and – most important to the future growth – ample woodland nearby for timber and fuel.

Birmingham's rateable value today is more than £55,000,000. In the Domesday Survey of 1086 it was worth twenty shillings, with land enough for six ploughs.

For 400 years Birmingham grew slowly. Even so, by 1400, the first few craftsmen were among the earliest lists of taxpayers and the pattern of the Birmingham to come was beginning to emerge like the first tentative outlines on an artist's sketch pad. Already there were Upper and Lower Priory, Bull Street, the village market place of the Bull Ring and the first St. Martin's Church. Most of the main roads leading out of the city today to Coventry, Warwick, Stratford, Dudley, Walsall and Stafford, existed in crude form.

By now, too, the traditional dependence on the soil was being supplemented by the growth of metal working and by tanning and textile manufacture. To north and south villages had what Birmingham wanted to make use of: sand, wood, wool, coal, leather, grain. To do trade with each other, the groups of villagers came to Birmingham crossing the river in Deritend when they had to – and if they could, since there was perpetual mud and frequent flooding.

Transport of heavier and bulkier goods was gradually becoming possible and Birmingham was emerging as the hub of a road network. From being one of the smaller villages, it outgrew its neighbours because the habit had grown of going to market in Birmingham.

Another attraction which helped the growth of the village was the ready availability of land on which a man could set himself up as an independent craftsman, doubling as an agricultural worker, or as a merchant.

In the early part of the 16th century an important new area of iron manufacturing grew up along the valley of the River Tame, prompted again by the nearness of the market and available supplies of fuel – wood from Perry Manor woods – and water.

The map of 1553 on page 16 shows that the centre of Birmingham had already started to shift away from St. Martin's and up the hill. New Street, High Street, Park Street, Moore Street (then Molle Street) and Bennett's Hill can all be seen. The move up the hill was because, not surprisingly, the better land along the southern slopes belonged to the Manor, who retained it for their own profit until the early 18th century. Within the Manor at that time were a malt mill and two corn mills, plenty of agricultural land and numerous smithies.

However, the de Berminghams had acquired land elsewhere and seemed to show little or no interest in the Manor or the manor house, which fell into decay. In 1533 Edward de Bermingham forfeit his lands, the priory, gilds and chantries which had been established were dissolved and in many respects the people were able to take more power into their own hands and enjoy a large measure of freedom and independence.

It was an independence which was to show itself in various forms in the years to come: in the Church and King riots, the Chartist riots, the No-Popery riots, and it was something which was to earn the 'Brummie' a

...utation for a certain streak of cussedness.

During the Civil War, Birmingham supported the forces of Parliament, supplying some 15,000 sword blades. In 1642, Charles I, en route from Shrewsbury to Banbury, had his baggage, coin and plates seized by the townspeople, who handed it over to the Parliamentary garrison at Warwick. Before the Battle of Edgehill, the King rested at Aston Hall, which was beseiged by the people and still bears the marks.

The owner, Sir Thomas Holte, was heavily fined by the town for his royal support but in revenge Prince Rupert's forces made camp the following year on Camp Hill, attacked the town, plundered and burned much of it and subsequently levied a staggering fine of £30,000.

After the Restoration the town had a period of intense economic activity and became the centre for the manufacture of toys (not playthings but trinkets and small metal objects), buckles and guns. Steel houses were set up in what was then White Hall Lane but soon became Steelhouse Lane and smithies were to be found in all the main streets.

By 1700 the population had increased enormously, some estimates putting it as high as 15,000. It is unlikely that the increase was due to a migration of poor people since the Act of Settlement of 1662 had provided that if they seemed unable to offer sufficient security against becoming a burden on the local poor rate they could be bundled back from whence they came within 40 days. More probably, Birmingham was attracting increasing numbers of craftsmen, merchants and traders.

Tanning and cloth making were still, in 1700, playing an important role but the seeds of the Industrial Revolution had already been sown and were soon to put out their first shoots in Birmingham.

The town was already an industrial, a commercial and a trading centre. Coupled with its own, home-grown prosperity was the flourishing South Staffordshire coalfield on its borders, providing good fuel for the smiths and cutlers. The Black Country's sandstone quarries were supplying coarse grindstones for the edge tool industry and pig-iron refined in Cannock and the forges on the northern fringes of the area was finding a growing Birmingham market.

Demand for houses was great and the spread northwards from St. Martin's continued, while houses in the old centre were converted or extended to take more families.

St. Philip's was built and consecrated in 1715 and Old Square and Temple Row became the fashionable areas for leading manufacturers and merchants to live.

By 1731 the population had risen to an estimated 23,000 and the most prosperous trades were based on iron, while leather and textiles continued to decline in importance. Swords, nails and edge tools surpassed textiles and tanning and the smiths and cutlers came to represent the middle range of importance.

Another section of industry relying on metal was also growing: the manufacture of guns, buttons, toys and brass articles. This was later to become the dominant section of industry as the emphasis shifted from reliance on easily available sources of power – water, coal and charcoal – to a reliance on skills in using the available raw materials to the best advantage.

Colonial trade brought a wider market for the gunsmiths and the fashion at home and abroad for hats, breeches and shoes sporting buckles brought prosperity to these manufacturers.

At the same time wholesale and retail merchants were gaining in importance and many ironmongers acted as moneylenders – from which later came the town's recognition as a banking centre. The printers and

By the end of the 16th century Birmingham products, including bows, swords and daggers – the start of the arms trade – were finding markets in many parts of the country. There were also about 20 firms involved in large scale trade, including several mercers who imported textiles not easily available nearby and who gave their name to Mercer Street (later to become Spiceal Street because of the important trade in spices).

*In the 16th and 17th centuries Birmingham made blades for this type of sword.*

In 1762, Matthew Boulton's famous Soho Manufactory was established on waste land in Handsworth Heath with power from Hockley Brook. It was here that the prolific partnership of Boulton and James Watt was joined in 1774 and here that steam engines chugged out the power to produce toys, trinkets and plated goods of all kinds. This partnership was, perhaps, typical of the way in which Birmingham's growth to prosperity was engineered – by a combination of local craft and imported skill. Boulton was the son of a Snow Hill metal worker; Watt was born in Greenock and was a mathematical instrument maker before becoming interested in steam in 1763. The two were joined by the Ayrshire-born and equally inventive William Murdock in 1777.

*Boulton, Watt, and Murdock, the three Birmingham-based men who made the industrial revolution possible.*

booksellers who were to become a feature of the town's cultural life were gathering about High Street and the first newspaper, Aris's Gazette, was published in 1741.

By 1750 the lower town and Digbeth possessed retail premises, many inns, workshops and a slitting mill. Park Street and Moor Street were heavily built upon and building had extended also along Snow Hill. The New Hall Estate was developing on land which had been the mansion and park of the Colmore family. This new, neatly laid-out estate included both fine houses for the prosperous and workshops for migrant and locally-expanding manufacturers of toys, buttons and buckles.

The hall itself became Matthew Boulton's warehouse. Soon afterwards the nearby estate of Sir Thomas Gooch around the Coleshill Road was similarly developed. To Weaman Street went the gunsmiths, prospering thanks to Continental wars and a growing trade in the new sporting guns. The small family workshop began to disappear to be replaced by large manufactories.

With the combined skills of Boulton, Watt, and Murdock Birmingham saw the introduction of the letter-copying press, the double-action steam engine, the rotative engine, public gas lighting and the coining press which produced Britain's first copper coinage and was used by Birmingham Mint for over a century.

Under their example the quality of Birmingham's products improved considerably and the town entered the market for jewellery and plated goods.

The introduction of plating was due to John Taylor, who applied it to buttons and trinkets and whose ingenuity and business acumen seemed boundless.

Ingenuity and invention, adaptation and improvement – these were the keynotes of the chord which Birmingham struck. Enamelling, japanning and the invention of papier mâché, tube-drawing, 'ingenious mechanical contrivances', brass work of all kinds, metal for everything imaginable from pots and pans to statuettes – these were just some of the things which were to make the mark 'Made in Birmingham' known all over the world.

In 1768 the Birmingham Canal was opened, to be followed in 1770 by the growing network which would connect land-locked Birmingham with the Thames, the Trent, the Humber, the Mersey and the Severn and which brought the great advantages of low transportation costs and gave a new dimension to the town.

New ironworks and coal mines in the neighbourhood were given financial backing by the recently established banks, including Taylors and Lloyds (now Lloyds Bank) and by 1773 the Assay Office was set up and the first of what were to become the building societies were advancing money.

Now people were flocking to the town; not just craftsmen and merchants but lawyers, surgeons, teachers, writers, architects, artists and actors.

Baskerville was designing his founts of type and publishing his beautiful volumes; William Hutton was writing *An History of Birmingham*; Sketchley was compiling his first *Directory of Birmingham*.

Lichfield's native Dr. Johnson, who had lived for a time in the town and had friends among the printers and booksellers, might look scathingly on the town and say that in Lichfield 'we are a city of philosophers; we work with our heads and make the boobies of Birmingham work for us with their hands,' but a cultural life was growing amongst the commerce.

By 1800 the Birmingham Library had grown from a mere corner cupboard in a house in Snow Hill to occupy its own specially designed building. In 1774 a new theatre of standing was seeking a licence but

urke, reflecting some of the cultural snobbery of Johnson and believing
e town not worthy of real theatre – though good quality drama was
ready being performed there – said in Parliament: 'I look upon
rmingham to be the great toy shop of Europe'. The theatre, to become
e Theatre Royal in New Street, was not finally licensed until 1807.

The Triennial Music Festivals held to raise money for the General
ospital were established in 1784 and offered performances of the highest
der.

In 1791 the town's reputation was tarnished by the Church and
ing riots centering on Joseph Priestley and the agitation for relief from
litical and religious encumbrances. The New Meeting House, Priestley's
vn house and laboratory in Sparkbrook and William Hutton's house
d library were burned down by militant Church members and Tories
fore troops restored order. Four riot leaders were hanged and the
ssenters were reimbursed.

Priestley himself fled to London and later to America to escape
ntinuing persecution, losing to the town's Lunar Society one of its most
noured members.

The Society was founded about 1766, its principal members originally
ing Boulton, Dr. Erasmus Darwin and the physician and chemist
r. William Small, later to be joined by Watt, the chemist James Keir,
siah Wedgwood, the philosopher Richard Lovell Edgeworth, the
tanist and chemist Dr. William Withering, Murdock and Priestley.

The idea in itself was not original and has been repeated many times
nce – good food, good wine and good talk but the mixture of members
as such that from their gatherings (held on the Monday nearest each full
oon) flowed scientific theory, inventiveness, political and religious
ncepts which had far-reaching consequences, and which helped establish
e town as an industrial and commercial centre of national note.

After the 1791 riots the Society gradually broke down and by the end
f the century only Keir, Boulton and Watt remained. The latter,
cidentally, leased Aston Hall after the death of Sir Charles Holte, until
is own death in 1848, when it was bought for the town.

The population of the town, 70,000 in 1801, continued to grow and by
831 was 130,000. Thirty years later it was 300,000 and there were quite
ensely populated strips and pockets from Handsworth down to Balsall
eath and from Harborne over to Saltley, though there was still plenty
f open space and 'real countryside'. Edgbaston's purely residential
althorpe Estate was matched by the superior character of fashionable
slington.

In the first sixty years of the 19th century there was another change in
e manufacturing emphasis of Birmingham: guns, jewellery, buttons and
rass products were now the staple industries, the jewellers concentrating
ventually around Vyse Street and Warstone Lane, the 'Jewellery
uarter'. The button trade took on a 'new look' with bone, glass, ivory
nd pearl covered buttons. The brass trade, recovering from a depression,
evived and stabilised, branching into naval brass, plumbing and cabinet
ttings, wire and lamps, gas and carriage fittings and brass bedsteads.

In less than 20 years the town became the centre of a railway network
ith the opening first of the Birmingham-Liverpool line in 1837, followed
year later by the London line from Curzon Street. By the early 1850s
ew Street and Snow Hill had main line stations in addition to Curzon
treet and Moor Street.

Tubes for railway locomotives were added to the other new metal skills:
inges, fire irons, fenders and grates, wood screws and steel pens.

In 1813 a Chamber of Commerce was formed and in 1834 the new covered

Boosted by the American Civil War from
1861 to 1865, the gun trade thrived. Close
on 800,000 guns were exported to America.
The practice of group trading by gunsmiths
had begun in 1689 when William III
placed five of the town's gunmakers under
contract to supply 200 muskets a month at
17 shillings a piece. The practice led to
the formation of the Birmingham Small
Arms Trade Association, which became the
B.S.A. Co. Ltd. in 1861.
*Short Enfield muzzle loading rifles were made
at Small Heath by the Birmingham Small Arms
Company and used extensively in the American
Civil War.*

Joseph Chamberlain was elected to the Council in 1869 and was Mayor from 1873-75. By 1874 he had made enough money to devote most of his time to Radical politics and worked ceaselessly to improve his adoptive town. In 1876 he joined John Bright to represent the borough in Parliament. His younger son, Neville, was to become Lord Mayor in 1915-17 and Prime Minister from 1937 to 1940.
*Joseph Chamberlain, 1836-1914.*

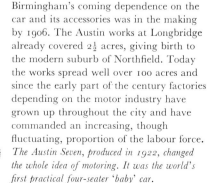

Birmingham's coming dependence on the car and its accessories was in the making by 1906. The Austin works at Longbridge already covered 2½ acres, giving birth to the modern suburb of Northfield. Today the works spread well over 100 acres and since the early part of the century factories depending on the motor industry have grown up throughout the city and have commanded an increasing, though fluctuating, proportion of the labour force.
*The Austin Seven, produced in 1922, changed the whole idea of motoring. It was the world's first practical four-seater 'baby' car.*

market hall and the Town Hall opened. In 1832 the Reform Act saw the town's elevation to a parliamentary borough after its people had played a leading role, under Thomas Attwood, in agitating for reform. The first council of 16 aldermen and 48 councillors from 13 wards was elected that December. Six years later came the Charter of Incorporation and in 1851 the Improvement Act constituted the corporation as the sole municipal authority.

The Council House was built on land adjacent to the Town Hall bought by the Commissioners for Streets and townspeople and was opened in 1879, thus shifting the centre of administration, such as it had been until then, from the area of St. Martin's, where the Commission had set up offices in 1807.

Though Birmingham was at this time claiming to have air which was 'naturally exceeding pure' and to be one of the healthiest towns in Britain, sanitation and public health were minimal and probably not helped by a pig population which was assessed at 3,210 and caused a not inconsiderable nuisance. The main streets had underground drains but areas such as Deritend and Bordesley had only open sewers in front of the houses.

From the middle of the 19th century the pattern of industry again changed with natural development along the lines of railways and canals and pockets or strips of industrial growth springing up at Ladywood, Selly Oak, Stirchley, Tyseley, Washwood Heath and Witton.

Bournville came into being and was developed as a model village after the Cadbury brothers had moved out of their cocoa and chocolate making factory in Bridge Street in 1879.

Other new industries coming into being were metal-based: bicycles, cars and electrical goods. The most important development in this latter field was the erection of The General Electric Company's works at Witton in 1901.

Now, too, began the intensive residential in-filling in areas all round the city. The building of Corporation Street between 1878 and 1882 swept away a notoriously unsalubrious area of the city centre – thanks largely to the efforts of Joseph Chamberlain – and the people from this and other central crowded areas began to settle in the new suburbs.

In 1888 the town became a county borough and a year later at last gained city status. Seven years on and the title of Lord Mayor was first conferred on its chief magistrate, by which time the city's bounding boundary extensions were under way, culminating in Aston Manor, Handsworth, King's Norton, Northfield, Yardley and Erdington becoming part of the city under the Greater Birmingham Scheme of 1911. Though this enabled a proper co-ordination of local services for the first time, Birmingham was in danger of outstripping itself.

House building was not keeping pace with the population increase, water demand was outpacing local supply – the Elan Valley scheme to carry water from the Welsh valleys resulted in 1891 and was inaugurated in 1904 – and the city was an extraordinary mixture of mean houses, jumbled streets, factories and neatly laid-out newer suburbs.

The turn of the century saw the incorporation of Birmingham University absorbing Mason College which had been endowed by Sir Josiah Mason the pen manufacturer thirty years earlier. In 1904 the Bishopric and Diocese of Birmingham were created.

Speculative residential building was spreading a belt around most of the city and attracting population from its centre. Then, in 1909, the Town Planning Act, the first in the country, was passed, giving the local authority its first real control over the development of the city.

The 1914-18 war interrupted the strides being made in the civic life but brought intense industrial activity as the city poured out guns and ammunition, armour and vehicles in addition to its men. To promote the great drive for war savings, the Municipal Bank was set up in 1916 and established on a permanent basis in 1919.

A brief period of phoney boom after the war was followed by the lowering clouds of depression which hung over the city for years, though it suffered less than many. Even so, from 1919 to the start of the Second World War vast progress was made both civically – in planning, hospitals, health, education, slum clearance, for example – and culturally – in the City of Birmingham Orchestra (now the C.B.S.O.), the widening reputation of the Repertory Theatre under Barry Jackson, the great extension of activities by the Midland Institute which had been instituted as long ago as 1854, and in the Barber Institute of Fine Arts.

Again war plunged Birmingham into hectic activity in the production of arms, ammunition, aircraft, vehicles and all the equipment of war. This time, though, the war was brought to the rooftops by German raiders which inflicted heavy damage and casualties.

The market hall was reduced to a shell but from it grew today's vast Bull Ring Centre, built at a cost of £8-million and opened in 1964.

Enormous advances have been made in sweeping away the slums, many of which were blasted by bombs to begin the clearance. The people from the slum areas moved to new tall flats or modern council houses in the city or spilled over to new towns.

The first section of the Inner Ring Road opened in 1960 and today the modern Queensway throws a convenient belt for traffic around the centre. The Claerwen Dam extension of the Welsh water scheme was inaugurated in 1952 and 1961 saw the completion of the scheme. In 1966 Aston's College of Advanced Technology received university status and became The University of Aston in Birmingham.

In the following year the modern New Street Station was officially opened, after prolonged and almost total rebuilding, to coincide with electrification. After being an important rail centre, the city now has just one main line station; Snow Hill is derelict and Moor Street skeletonised. Instead, the city is again the hub for road transport as the centre of the country's motorway system. The working canals have given place to canal cruises and walkways. From the timbered village and the brick town, Birmingham has become a concrete city. With local government reform vast changes are taking place physically and administratively. Over the future of the city hangs a question mark – but even that will surely be metal-based.

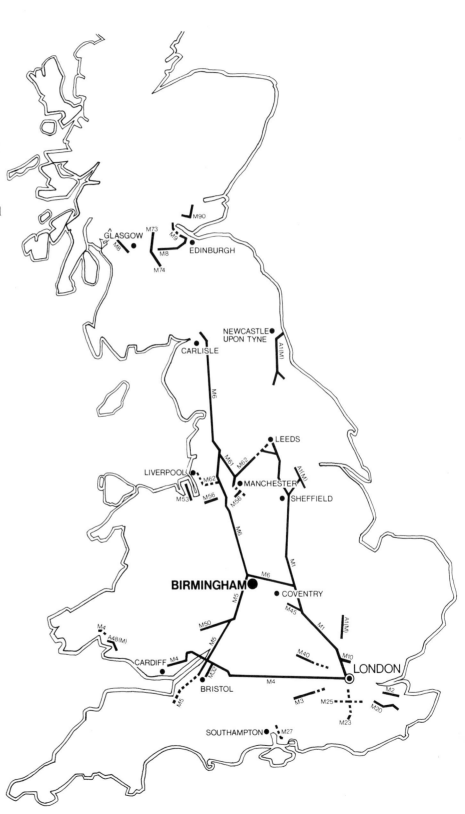

*Birmingham, the centre of Britain's motorway system.*

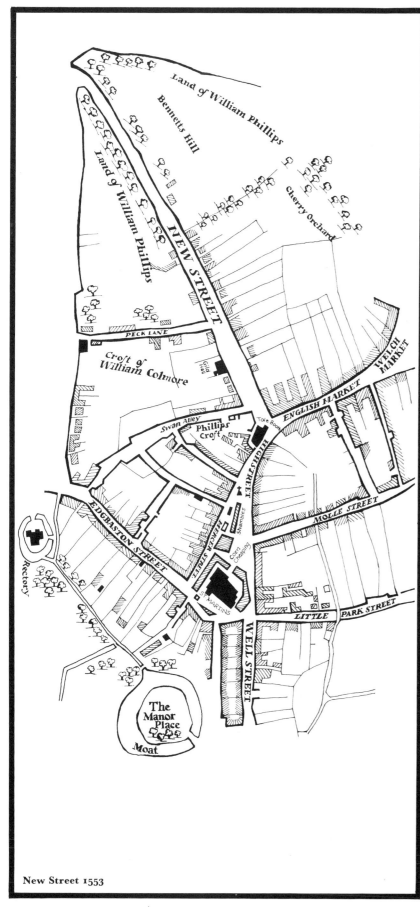

New Street 1553

## Development of New Street
Drawing and commentary by
John Broadhurst

### New Street 1553
At this time Birmingham was referred to as a Manor. The Bull Ring and New Street were the main thoroughfares, the dwellings being situated along the frontages. The land behind was either grassland or orchards which in some cases were owned by free tenants and gilds. The majority of the land was, however, owned by local notaries. St. Martin's was the parish church.
The Manor Place and its moat – the ancient seat of the de Bermingham family – holds a dominant position at the south-east entrance to Birmingham. (Re-drawn from a section of the conjectural plan of Birmingham, 1553.)

### New Street 1875
The town centre was now much enlarged and the inhabitants had spread out farther than in the map of 1553.

What was once fields was completely covered with buildings. Although the direction and position of New Street remains the same, side streets have sprung from it – each with its own collection of shops, offices, hotels and banks mainly in Victorian styles.

A predominant scar on the face of Birmingham was about to be removed with the building of a new road (Corporation Street). This was to cut through an area of doubtful repute (described in Council plans as 'the unhealthy area'), created by the conditions of the industrial revolution. The market hall had extended the area of trading in the Bull Ring and immediately behind it was the London & North Western Railway Station. (Re-drawn from the street plan of the Birmingham Improvement Scheme, 1875.)

### New Street 1972
Compared with the map of 1875 the market hall has been replaced with a huge shopping complex. New Street Station has been completely re-built and is now amongst the most modern railway stations in the world.

The granite setts of the 19th century have given way to the ringways of the 20th.

Amidst all this, New Street still stands – its course practically unchanged. It has been suggested that in the future it may become a pedestrian area.

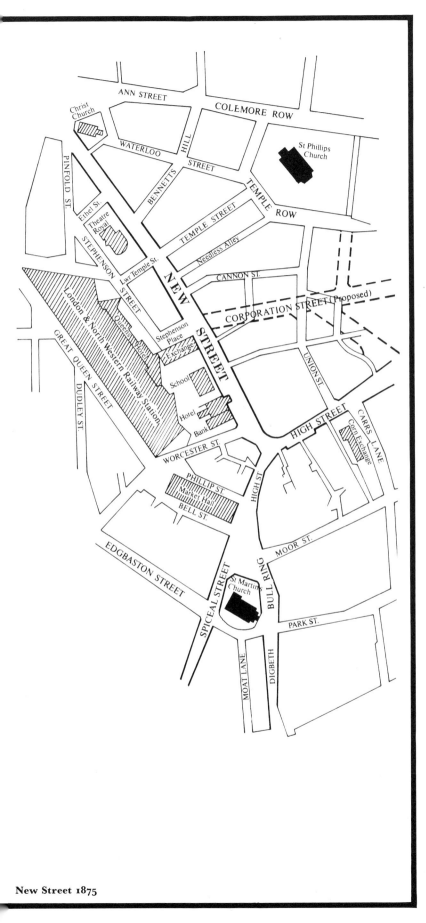

**New Street 1875**

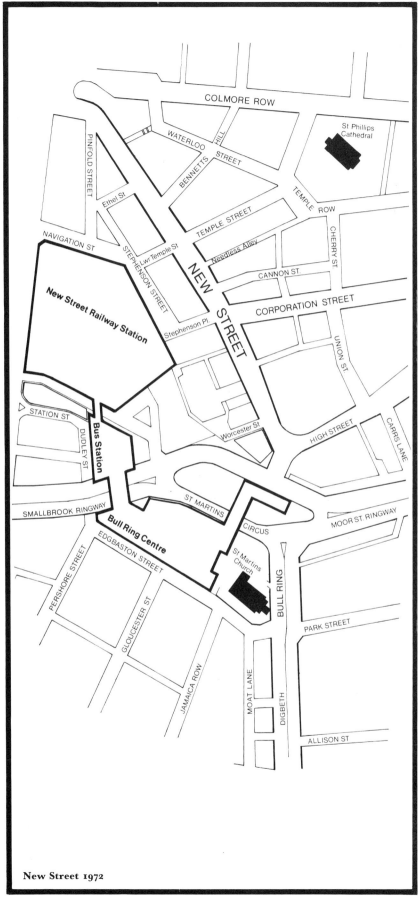

**New Street 1972**

# Victorian Photographers

by Edward Martin

*Thomas Lewis (1844-1913). Below: his signature and visiting card.*

THOMAS · LEWIS,

**Photographer,**

(Speciality: Manufacturers' Patterns, Cycle Manufacturers, Brassfounders, Engineers, &c.),

MERTON HOUSE, 200, STRATFORD ROAD,

BIRMINGHAM.

Photography is just 150 years old. Before its discovery, mathematical optics was an established science, the darkening action of light on some silver salts was known, and there had been cameras, of sorts. However, it was not until one bright spring day in 1822 that a camera was pointed at a subject and its image formed upon a surface capable of retaining permanently what the lens had seen. The place was Gras, Saint-Loup-de-Varennes, near Châlon-sur-Sâone, 200 miles south-east of Paris. The inventor – Joseph Nicéphore Nièpce.

The monumental efforts of Nièpce (1765-1833) were overshadowed by Louis Jacques Mandé Daguerre (1789-1851), who improved the process and launched the Daguerreotype. This swept the world and endowed Daguerre with fame and fortune. It brought portraiture to the masses and made even humble folk seem immortal.

Daguerreotypes yielded beautifully detailed, delicate images on silver-plated copper but they were laterally reversed, had to be viewed at critical angles, and could not be reproduced in quantity. With such limitations, the Daguerreotype set a pace, but was rapidly overtaken.

During Victorian times Britain established a lead not only in the manufacture of photographic equipment, but in processing. In 1839, at Laycock Abbey, Wiltshire, William Henry Fox Talbot (1800-1877) had independently produced a negative from which any number of paper prints could be made. The photograph had arrived. The Calotype, as it was called, prompted some of the finest photography the world has seen. It is a debatable point that whilst there were a handful of brilliant photographers in Victorian England, still only a handful exist today.

Victorian photography at its best has to be experienced to be believed: Fox Talbot's precise records; the deep, mysterious portraits by Julia Margaret Cameron; and the history of the times captured by Hill and Adamson, Frank Sutcliffe, and Roger Fenton – all are outstanding. Every square inch of a good photograph is relevant. Look closely at the pictures in this book. Because cameras were cumbersome and glass plates heavy and expensive, photographers thought hard before each exposure. There was time to love photography.

Thomas Lewis (1844-1913) lived in Moor Street, Birmingham, next door to Pickering and Stern, 'photographic artists'. As a schoolboy he must have been fascinated by what he saw. The draped studio relied on a large window, good weather, and clients being punctual to catch the best light. On a stand was the camera, made of wood and possibly of the sliding-box type, for bellows had achieved little popularity in England by the 1860s. A hand-painted landscape rolled down behind a low mock-garden wall, and the props of the time stood around: a small Doric column, chairs with headrests to prevent sitters' heads moving during the long exposure times, and a few tasteful house plants completing the clutter. No doubt Thomas would also peer into the coloured gloom of the darkroom and would catch the smell of candles burning in the safelights. The distinctive pungency of collodion being carefully run across glass plates added a magical touch to the new alchemy. In comparison the prospect of perpetuating his father's tailoring business seemed just a little dull.

Ten years later photography was off on another gallop. Stereoscopic photography, almost overnight, became a craze which in England equalled the first wave of the Daguerreotype.

To a pre-automobile Birmingham, regular holidays were a dream. Instead, the stereoscope became a magic carpet. It enabled people to cross the Channel and the oceans, gaze at Europe, the Americas and legendary India with a detail akin to a personal visit. The world, its

ltures, and the possessive satisfaction of seeing Britain's overseas
mains gripped Victorians. Photographers were busy, often prosperous
ople, whose expeditions brought the world to the drawing-room. If
iddle-class Britain was romantic, photographers were dramatic, integral
th every move of the advancing civilisation. The variety of such an
cupation beckoned many a young soul, as it still does today.

Then there was the lantern slide. The church was quick to use the magic
ntern – a visual aid as important as the former illuminated manuscripts.
ie Holy Land and the travels and work of missionaries were topics as
pular as slide-stories from the Bible. An afternoon at Sunday School
thout a magic lantern was considered a bore.

Thomas Lewis, at the age of twenty-five, opened his first studio, in Moor
reet in 1871. A year later he moved to better premises in up-town
iradise Street. This foundered with the increasing overheads the expensive
e demanded. Then for five years Lewis was a photographer for the
mous view-card firm of Frith and Sons. He travelled the whole of Great
itain, and acquired a feeling for views which was to remain with him all
rough his life. He learned what to include in a scene and what to leave out.
l 1879 he set up in business on his own again and this time he succeeded.
ewis photographed many of Birmingham's expanding industries and
came one of the country's first commercial and architectural
iotographers, along with Bedford le Mare of London and Stewart Bale
'Liverpool. In 1894 he moved to 200 Stratford Road, Sparkbrook. The
isiness is still there.

The majority of Victorian artists were portrait and miniature painters.
ith the advent of the Daguerreotype, miniature painting died all too
iickly, and many artists changed over to photography. The artist-turned-
iotographer was often successful. The themes of Victorian painting
fluenced the photography produced by such refugees. In the mid-1850s
enry Peach Robinson led a school which made photographs look more
ke paintings; his landscapes vied with those of James Mudd for their
iinterly qualities. Processes were invented which aided this affinity. The
omoil process, for example, relied upon the image actually being made
sible by pigment applied with a brush, and areas could be left light,
ippled-in darker, or even replaced. Another process, carbon printing,
as not only relatively simple – one could use almost any good quality
iper for the print – but it was permanent and beautiful.

Carbon printing became a speciality of the Whitlock studio, founded in
342 by Joseph Whitlock (1806-1857). Joseph was succeeded by his son
enry Joseph (1834-1918), his grandson – another Henry Joseph (1871-
)46) – and finally his great-grandson David Henry Whitlock (b. 1908).
hus the firm in New Street, and later in Corporation Street, saw the
hole history of portrait and group photography until the studio, along
ith many others, ceased operation in the 1960s.

Whitlock's was *the* place in Birmingham at which to be photographed.
hey received a flow of famous visitors, civic dignitaries, and even Royalty.
n special occasions Whitlock and Lewis joined forces; in 1897 they
ipplied an album for Queen Victoria of her Diamond Jubilee
elebrations in Birmingham.

Victorian photographers were apprenticed or self-taught. Today, in
:hools of photography such as we have in modern Birmingham, students
om the world over are produced who photograph in colour, make films
ir television, and explore creation in wavelengths undetectable to the eye.
irmingham and photography have advanced together.

*Henry Joseph Whitlock (1834-1918).*
*Below: A letter of thanks from Mr. Gladstone.*

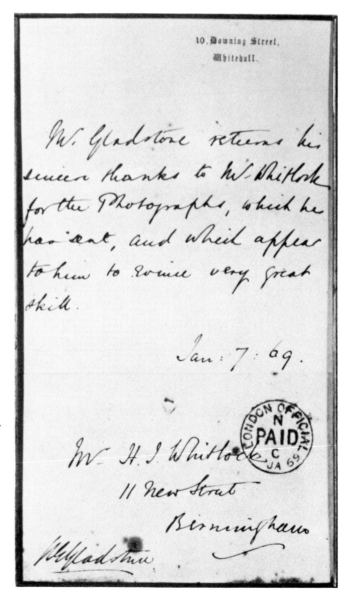

Towards the end of the 19th
century a short, bearded man could
often be seen diverting traffic. His
wave of the hand was peremptory.
He was concentrating on
photographing Birmingham.

His camera was made of
mahogany and bound in brass. The
8-inch by 10-inch glass plates,
protected in wooden darkslides,
also brass-bound, were stacked in a
leather bag beside him.

The man who had to manœuvre
this load was Thomas Lewis,
founder of John Whybrow Limited.
It was Lewis who initiated the
collection, a treasury of over 1,000
negatives and prints of Birmingham
taken between 1871 and 1930.
Each year, hundreds of modern
shots are added to give a
comprehensive gallery of the
city's growth.

Lewis set up his first studio at 18
Moor Street in 1871, but he changed
premises several times before the
business began to expand, about
1885, to include commercial,
industrial and architectural
photography. There was a trade,
too, in country scenes, some of which
were coloured by Thomas' wife,
Jane. This gave rise to a popular
venture in coloured portraits,
selling at a shilling, of Gladstone,
John Bright, Joseph Chamberlain
and other well-known people whom
Lewis photographed in their
own homes.

In 1894 Lewis made his final
move, to Merton House, 200
Stratford Road, Sparkbrook, where
three years later he was joined by
Roland George Randall.

In the late 1890s a Bromsgrove
branch of the firm existed, starting

from a market stall and
subsequently moving to studios in
the building of The Bromsgrove
Messenger. Here local forensic
history was made when a criminal's
fingerprints were photographed for
police records.

The commercial side of the firm
continued to expand through
contracts with important firms such
as Cadbury's, Henry Hope's of
Smethwick, and The General
Electric Company Limited
of Witton.

Lewis was partly helped in buying
new equipment by compensation
of £800 for a head injury sustained
when a steam-hauled tram
overturned at Camp Hill in the
early 1900s.

In 1913 Lewis engaged a new
photographer, Sidney Herbert
Edward Whybrow, father of John
Whybrow. A few months later
Lewis tripped down the stairs – it
was another tram – fractured his
skull, and died. Thomas Lewis is
remembered as a kindly, genial
man, a staunch Baptist, and an
outstanding photographer.

The firm continued, under the
direction of R. G. Randall.
S. H. E. Whybrow went away to the
1914-18 war, and returned. In 1919
the company changed its name to
Lewis & Randall Limited. Trade,
which had slumped during the war,
revived and exceeded pre-war
levels. Photographers, of which
S. H. E. Whybrow was now the
senior, visited dockyards, factories,
coalmines, churches and castles. In
1938 Randall retired and Whybrow
took control.

During the Second World War
the premises had several narrow

escapes: once, the building was hit
by incendiaries and Mr. Whybrow
and his son John, who would be
joining the company in 1947,
fought the blaze. On another
occasion high explosives straddled
the studios. The old glass negatives
survived unbroken.

In 1953 S. H. E. Whybrow
retired and John Whybrow became
managing director. In 1962 the
collection was expanded when the
120-year-old studios of H. J.
Whitlock & Sons Limited closed
and several hundred of Victorian
and Edwardian negatives
were acquired.

On the death of his father in
1968 John Whybrow took over the
business and its name was changed
to John Whybrow Limited two
years later.

The collection was given its
public showing in 1972 when 40 of
its selected photographs of city
scenes were compared with their
modern settings. Produced,
constructed and designed by the
Whybrow team, the exhibition
attracted enormous interest when
it was mounted at The Birmingham
Post. It was this interest from
elderly, middle-aged and young
people alike which gave rise to
this book.

# The Photographs 1857–1885

**Commentaries by Douglas Hickman**

## H22 High Street, Deritend, The Old Crown, c. 1857

Birmingham's oldest surviving pub, originally a mansion reputed to date from 1368. The bulk of the structure is probably 16th century and is remarkable for its simplicity of outline, the roof with its slightly bowed ridge being rather like the inverted hull of a boat. The construction is of close-set timber framing with wattle and daub infill and the main gables are carved with interlaced arcading. Originally the ground floor contained a central 'hall' w a smaller room at each end and four roo above plus the 'Gallorye Chamber' unde the projecting centre gable. The more recent incidental details in this photogra are intriguing—a bracketed lamp probal the work of the local blacksmith—an Ol Crown Inn sign looking more like an old hatchment—fire signs in the gables—an advertisement for Livery and Bait Stabli

-a Regency bow window on the ground
floor—a cobbled pavement laid in three
bands—a cannon bollard and a gentleman
in a stove pipe hat completing a Dickensian
scene. This is the oldest photograph in the
John Whybrow Collection. The negative,
still in fine condition, is possibly the
earliest surviving glass plate of a
Birmingham street scene.

## H672 High Street, Deritend, The Old Crown, 1971.

Most of the interesting incidental details
added before 1857 were removed during the
early 1860s. During 1851, 1856 and 1862
attempts were made to demolish the
building in the name of street improvements.
In 1862 the house was restored by Toulmin
Smith, a barrister, 'to more of the likeness
which it bore in the days of its youth than
it has had for some centuries'. In fact the
larger windows inserted on the ground floor
are out of character. This is now the only
half-timbered building in Deritend and
looks out of place alongside the dual
carriageway. Surely some more interesting
paving could be provided in sympathy with
the building? The railway viaduct in the
background is a magnificent example of
engineering in blue brick.

**H38 Stratford Road, Sparkhill, The Mermaid, 1873.**

This house at the fork of Warwick Road is mainly 18th century but can be traced back to 1675. It became a pub and was first described as The Mermaid in a lease dated 1751. In 1873 it is known as The Mermaid Inn and the licencee is G. Palmer. Note the pump, the timber horse troughs and the sign advertising the Tivoli Gardens.

**H39 Stratford Road, Sparkhill, The Mermaid, 1971.**

In 1895 the Mermaid Inn was rebuilt as the Mermaid Hotel with moulded brickwork and half-timbered gables, but the corner was damaged during World War II and subsequently rebuilt about 1949, to the design of the local architects Holland W. and M. A. H. Hobbiss, in the neo-Georgian style. **Left** Enlarged detail of H38.

## H45 Moseley Road, Moseley Village, c. 1875.

Moseley was a hamlet at the time of the Norman Conquest and belonged to the Manor of Bromsgrove. St. Mary's Church was originally built in 1496 in the parish of Kings Norton and the tower added in the early 16th century. This was replaced by a new church in 1780 and the tower partly refaced with brick, alterations being carried out by Thomas Rickman in 1823-4.

In 1875 Moseley is still a village. Tiled, red brick cottages and The Bull's Head next door to a shoeing forge front the village green.

## H722 Moseley Road, Moseley Village, 1971.

By the early 1900s Moseley had become a fashionable Birmingham suburb with a population of over 16,000. Many charming Art Nouveau houses were built on the Wake Green Road and the Salisbury Road, then recently cut through the landscaped grounds of Moseley Hall. The church was gradually rebuilt again by J. A. Chatwin and his son P. B. Chatwin from 1886 to 1910 and again in 1952-4 after war damage. The Bull's Head was rebuilt in the style of Norman Shaw, the doorways and bay windows strongly influenced by his New Zealand Chambers, Leadenhall Street, and was joined in the 1930s by a branch bank designed by Peacock and Bewlay.

The old footpath through to the churchyard has been retained. The houses to the left of this were replaced by shops with no attempt to provide an attractive side elevation.

The Fighting Cocks with the tower and the two adjoining shops were designed by T. W. F. Newton and Cheatle and are worth close study.

**H28 High Street, Deritend, c. 1885.**
On the left is the Golden Lion Inn, a pretty half-timbered building dating from about 1600 and very similar in design to Stratford House, Bordesley. Georgian sash windows have been ruthlessly cut into the herring-bone framework and the timber bracket over the footpath no longer holds the inn sign. The other houses date from the early 18th century but the nearer one, the Nelson Inn, has been refronted to conceal the roof and provided with sash windows. Both houses have been divided into two or more dwellings and considerably altered at ground floor level. St. John's Church, founded in 1381 as the Chapel of St. John the Baptist, was rebuilt in 1735 and is being restored. The square brick tower was built in 1762 and a chime of 'eight of the most musical bells' (Hutton) added in 1776.

**H727 High Street, Deritend, 1971.**
The facade of the Golden Lion Inn has been reconstructed in Cannon Hill Park. St. John's Church, damaged by enemy action in 1940, was demolished in 1947. The bells have now been hung in the Bishop Latimer Memorial Church, Handsworth. Thomas Haddon and Stokes' factory is about 17 feet further back than the altar of St. John's Church, the road having been widened on this side to provide a double carriageway. The new building is as dull as could be with the window heights decreasing towards the top, making the upper floors look unimportant.
A pompous two-storey porch shows the unfortunate influence of the Barber Institute of Fine Arts, Edgbaston.

**H50 Stratford Place, Bordesley,
Stratford House, c. 1880.**

Stratford House was built in 1601 for
Ambrose Rotton and his wife Bridget.
It is a typical Warwickshire half-timbered
building with close timber uprights at
ground-floor level, herring-bone timbering
at first-floor level and curved braces in the
gables; a formula adopted for Blakesley
Hall Yardley and the Golden Lion Inn
Deritend. The first-floor is jettied over the
ground-floor which has a later facing of
brick and the front garden is surrounded by
Gothic cast iron railings. There is a
tradition that Shakespeare stayed here and
that King Charles II spent the night hiding
in a space between the chimneys. Early in
the 19th century Stratford House was a
girls' school.

**H738 Stratford Place, Bordesley,
Stratford House, 1971.**

In 1926 Stratford House was threatened
with demolition to make way for improved
railway facilities. The Birmingham Civic
Society made every effort to persuade the
Corporation to restore the building but
failed to do so. The railway scheme was
halted by World War II but Stratford
House was vacated in 1945 because of
its doubtful condition. By 1950 the structure
was almost beyond repair and a second
appeal to the Corporation met with no
more response than the first. The architect,
James A. Roberts, however, was more
optimistic and carried out a miraculous
restoration which has enabled the building
to be used as offices.

**H57 Anderton Road, Sparkbrook, Green Stile Farm, c. 1880.**
The home of William Anderton who lived there in 1856. In 1896 it became James Shuter's builder's yard and was demolished shortly afterwards to make way for speculative housing. Fallows Road marched through the farmyard.

**H740 Anderton Road, Fallows Road, Sparkbrook, 1971.**
The Victorian speculative builder usually built terraces, reducing the width of his standard house to a minimum to enable a maximum number to be built on a site. There was no room for a hall and the view from the back parlour was down a narrow yard at the side of the scullery. A few 'artistic' details were usually added to the front wall but the cost of these would have been better spent on better planning. With this kind of development taking place it is not surprising that the Arts and Crafts Movement founded by William Morris had such a strong influence on Birmingham architects. W. Alexander Harvey, the architect of Bournville, despised 'the jerry-built house with its scroll-cut lintol and moulded string course' and thought ornament 'deprived dwellings of their homeliness'. Architects shunned style and argued that building should result from the application of the traditional rules of craftsmanship. They admired honest buildings like Green Stile Farm but these were being swept away as the city expanded.

**16 Moat Row, Smithfield Market, c. 1881.**

In the 12th century Peter de Bermingham had a moated manor house which, though rebuilt, survived complete with moat, along Moat Row, till the end of the 18th century. The photograph shows the open market, on the site of the manor house, which started in 1817 as a cattle market and later became a vegetable market. In 1881 the Smithfield Wholesale Fruit and Vegetable Market was built, on a site just off the left-hand side of the photograph, to the design of W. Spooner Till, the Borough Surveyor. This has brick outer walls, iron columns and a glass roof. The foundations had to be taken down to a depth of 14ft to get below the mud of the old moat. The Falcon steam tram is on its way to Small Heath.

**H741 Moat Row, Smithfield Market, 1971.**

The Drovers' Arms, a converted late 18th century house is still recognisable, though the top storey has been rebuilt without a cornice and the upper windows have lost their glazing bars. The characterful three dimensional lettering has disappeared and two of the acid-etched plate glass windows have been replaced by leaded lights. The Birmingham Arms, one of the city's best 'gin palaces', has also been tidied up at the expense of its original character by the removal of a vulgar dome and a wayward gable. The building on the extreme left is the 1903 extension to the Smithfield Wholesale Fruit and Vegetable Market, designed by F. B. Osborn. Smithfield House beyond, with bright red spandrel panels, was built in 1957 and designed by Llewellyn Smith and Waters of London. **Overleaf** Enlarged detail of H16

**H31 Corporation Street,
The Stork Hotel, c. 1883.**
The first Stork Hotel or Tavern was a few
yards away in Old Square but moved to
the Corporation Street/Lower Priory corner
when Corporation Street was constructed.
The new building designed in 1882 by
W. H. Ward, is in a French Renaissance
style with Second Empire details and faced
with stone. The carved panels at ground-
floor level are sensitively executed and the
projecting bays to the upper floors provide
modelling without destroying the general
form. On the right, a building, designed by
Martin and Chamberlain in 1883, is due
to be erected for Ray and Prosser,
paper-hanging dealers, which will go
through to Lower Priory at the back.

**H712 Corporation Street, Site of
Stork Hotel, 1971.**
Upper and Lower Priory have been mer
into the new Priory Ringway which cuts
across Corporation Street from Colmore
Circus to Masshouse Circus. The detaili
of Colonnade Developments by Frederic
Gibbard and Partners is refreshingly sim
compared with other new developments
the city, but lacks height and fails to
enclose the acres of surrounding tarmac.

**H19 High Street, Digbeth,
The Old Leather Bottle, c. 1885**

The Old Leather Bottle was built about
1625, possibly as two private houses and
its outline suggests that it may have a
timber frame. The sash windows and stucco
have been added at a later date in an
attempt to modernise the property.
The pavement and ground floor are 3-4 feet
lower than the street and often flooded by
the River Rea in winter.

**H711 High Street, Digbeth, 1972.**

The Old Leather Bottle closed down in
1891 and was then hidden from view for
years by advertisement hoardings. The new
building, which is quite out of scale with
the width of the new double carriageway,
does not make the most of the site as it lacks
upper floors to continue the general height
of the adjacent buildings. Revealed is the
glass roof of the former Birchley's
photographic portrait studios.

### H13 Corporation Street,
### The Grand Theatre, c. 1885.

This theatre, the largest of its kind in the town, was opened on November 14th, 1883. It was to be known as the 'New Theatre' but was soon called the 'Grand Theatre' and presented melodrama and opera at popular prices. The new building, designed by W. H. Ward, incorporates offices known as Assize and Old Square Chambers and the facade is in 'the style prevalent in France under the Second Empire', the mansard dome terminating in an allegorical group in metal. It is an accomplished design, though the ground floor is too broken up and the upper floors give the appearance of one building rising from behind another, due to the fact that there is a central pediment in addition to a central gable—the unfortunate influence of S. Etienne du Mont, Paris (facade 1620). The Gothic building on the left, the Birmingham Household Supply Association Limited, was designed by Martin and Chamberlain in 1880 and runs through to London Prentice Street at the back. The empty site on the right is to be occupied by the Central Wesleyan Chapel to be built about 1886-7 in the Early English Gothic style to the design of Osborn and Reading.

### H705 Corporation Street,
### Priory Ringway, 1971.

The theatre became the Grand Casino and the Chapel which continued in its original use for only 15 years became the Kings Hall Market. Both were demolished in the early 1960s to make way for the construction of Priory Ringway, part of a shortcut across the area within the inner ring road, from St. Chads Circus to Masshouse Circus, which deters pedestrians from shopping at this end of Corporation Street. Maples which replaces Martin and Chamberlain's Birmingham Household Supply Association is indecisive, but Colonnade Developments (housing Kean and Scott) by Frederick Gibberd and Partners is better with clear-cut stone elevations incised with vertical slots to give a grille effect. Lincoln's Inn Buildings (now Gazette Buildings), designed by W. H. Ward in 1882, has similarities in detail to the Colonnade Hotel in New Street but is a weak, confused design.

**H87 Stratford Road, Camp Hill, King Edward VI Grammar School, c. 1885.** During the Civil War in 1643 Camp Hill was the scene of a day's minor battle with Prince Rupert's forces. King Edward VI Grammar School for Boys, Camp Hill, was built in 1883 following a reform of the constitution of the former Free Grammar School in New Street, which became King Edward VI High School for Boys, and nearly half the original Camp Hill pupils came from the Middle School in New Street. The Camp Hill school was designed by the architects to the Birmingham School Board, Martin and Chamberlain who designed many schools in the Venetian Gothic style. This school is robust and well-detailed but, though it owes much to the work of William Butterfield, its form lacks vigour. A chimney sits timidly on the ridge of the main front gable rather than meet the rows of windows which defy its presence.

**H745 Stratford Road, Camp Hill, 1971.** The Girls' School, which started in a room over a boys' school in Meriden Street, Digbeth, was added in 1893. This confused the original composition and some very unsympathetic alterations and additions have taken place since. In 1956-8 the King Edward VI Schools at Camp Hill moved to Vicarage Road, Kings Heath, and the building is now Bordesley Teachers' Training College.

## H9 Joseph Chamberlain, c. 1885.

Joseph Chamberlain was born in London in 1836 and came to Birmingham in 1854 to join the family firm of Nettlefold and Chamberlain. Having established his fortune he became, in 1867, chairman of the National Education League which campaigned for free compulsory education. In 1868 he entered the Borough Council and was elected Mayor in 1873. Three years later Chamberlain entered Parliament as a Liberal, but, after a break with Gladstone over Home Rule in Ireland, became Colonial Secretary in the Conservative Government of 1895.

In 1873 Chamberlain had declared 'In twelve months by God's help the town will not know itself'. It took a little longer than that—but not much. He was appointed Mayor for a second term and in July 1875 he organised the Improvement Committee. This was to submit a scheme for the redevelopment of the large area of slums which had grown up around Old Square, Lichfield Street and Staniforth Street.

A great street—Corporation Street—'as broad as a Parisian Boulevard' must be driven through the area from New Street to the Aston Road. After considerable opposition a bill to confirm the scheme passed both Houses of Parliament and received the Royal Assent on 15th August, 1876.

The Improvement Scheme set the pace and thrust Birmingham in the fore front of municipal progress. By 1890 the American observer, J. Ralph, declared Birmingham to be 'the best governed city in the world'. No man had played a more constructive part in this achievement than Joseph Chamberlain. He died in 1914.

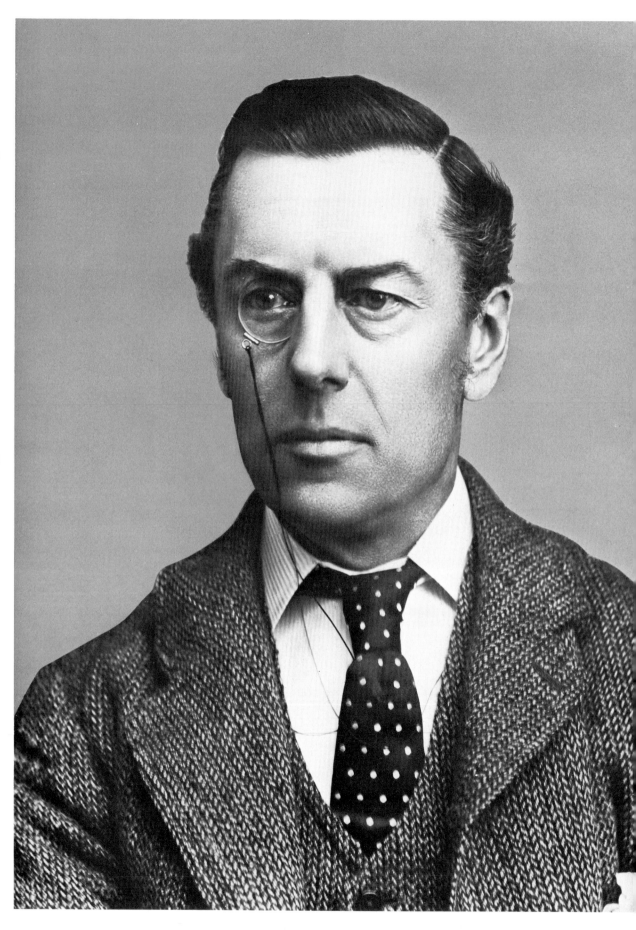

**H18 John Bright, c. 1885.**
John Bright was born in 1811 in Rochdale,
Lancs. He had a Quaker upbringing and
in 1840 launched with Richard Cobden
a campaign for the repeal of the corn laws.
In 1843 he entered Parliament and in 1857
became one of the Liberal M.Ps. for
Birmingham, launching a new campaign
for extension of franchise which helped to
bring about the Reform Act of 1867.
He was a famous orator who packed the
Town Hall and swayed audiences 'like
cornfields beneath the winds'. From 1868
onwards he was President of the Board of
Trade in several Liberal governments but
resigned from office in 1880 because of
Liberal policy in Egypt. When he died in
1888 he had been a Birmingham M.P.
for 31 years.

**H300 Aston Villa Football Club, 1887.**
The team, founded in 1874, had its origins in the Bible Class of Aston Villa Wesleyan Chapel and its first pitch was in Wellington Road, Perry Barr. The club turned professional in 1885. In 1887 they won the F.A. Challenge Cup, and again in 1895, 1897, 1905, 1913, 1920 and 1957—a record number of wins. The club moved to its present ground at Villa Park in 1896.
Back row: F. Coulton, J. Warner, F. Danson, An Unknown (reserve), J. Simmonds, Middle row: R. Davies, A. Brown, A. Hunter (Captain), H. Vaughan, D. Hodgetts.
Front: H. Yates, J. Burton.

**750 Aston Villa Football Club, 1971.**
he present club colours and design have
een worn since 1888. In 1972 Aston Villa
ained promotion to Division II of the
ootball League, whilst at the same time
irmingham City went up into Division I.
Photograph by courtesy of J. Weir, Esq.)
ack row: J. Brown, R. Graydon,
. Chatterley, A. Lochhead, M. Beard,
. Gibson, M. Wright.
Middle row: R. Rudge, L. Martin,

C. Aitken, G. Crudgington, F. Turnbull,
T. Hughes, G. Curtis, B. Rioch,
W. Anderson.
Front row: V. Crowe, B. Tiler, H. Gregory,
P. McMahon, I. Hamilton, N. Rioch,
K. Bradley, G. Vowden, R. Wylie.

**H23 Digbeth, Crowley's Court, c. 1887.**
This is one of a dozen similar courts erected in Georgian times between Floodgate Street and Cheapside showing a typical outside staircase. Through the small archway is probably High Street, Digbeth. Originally there was a coachway through the building, hence the surviving elliptical arch over the shuttered groundfloor window. The buildings are mid-Georgian with narrow glazing-bars to the windows but not with the concealed sashes usual for better quality work. The iron window-box holders indicate that the place was cared for at some time and the wrought iron lamp-holder converted for gas is an interesting detail. Thomas Crowley, born in 1799, was a well-known timber merchant at 48 Cheapside and founded an orphanage for poor girls in Edgbaston.

**H744 Digbeth, probable site of Crowley's Court, 1971.**
Green Street, just behind Digbeth, was built up with commercial and industrial premises, mainly in the late 1950s and early 1960s with facing-brick screen walls concealing utilitarian framed structures. How much more interesting it would be had the various structures been well designed and honestly expressed as industrial architecture.

**14 Upper Priory, Central Fire Station, c. 1890.**

The fire brigade was at first part of the police force with a fire station in Little Cannon Street equipped with five engines 1874. In 1879 the Brigade was made a separate body, with Alfred Robert Tozer Superintendent and in 1883 a Central Fire Station was built in Upper Priory, with accommodation for eleven married men. It was designed by the Birmingham architects Martin and Chamberlain and though John Henry Chamberlain died in 1883 he would have been responsible for the design which was carried out at about the same time as that for the School of Art. There are similarities between the two buildings, notably the projecting gables, but the Central Fire Station is appropriately more robust in appearance. It is a pity that the design is so street conscious with more decoration on the front than the side.

**H724 Priory Ringway, Site of the Central Fire Station, 1971.**

The Central Fire Station moved to Corporation Street in 1935 and No. 12, Priory Ringway, a block of shops and offices, was built on the site in the early 1960s. Could anything be more dull than these evenly spaced windows with every third upright concealing the supporting frame?

**H4 St. Philip's Place, The Blue Coat School, c. 1890.**

The Blue Coat School, founded in 1722, was built in 1724 on the eastern side of St. Philip's churchyard as a Church of England School to combat the 'profaneness and debauchery especially among the poorer sorts'. It was supported by regular twice-yearly contributions and collections made after sermons. In 1792-4 the building was greatly enlarged and improved and the elevations faced with stone by John Rawsthorne the architect of the ill-fated Crescent. About 200 children were clothed in blue and educated by a governor and governess until they were 14. On the right is Regent House, the residence of the rector of St. Philip's church, built in 1883 to the design of Osborn and Reading on the site of the original parsonage garden.

**H708 St. Philip's Place, Site of the Blue Coat School, 1971.**

The 18th century Blue Coat School building was demolished in 1935 and replaced by Prudential buildings, a Portland stone block of offices in a chaste classical style. The figures of charity children over the entrance to the old building are now in the entrance hall of the new Blue Coat School at Harborne. In the 1950s Regent House was extended upwards by three floors which include the Provost's Lodge. The original building became offices. The adjoining branch of the Bank of England, a robust classical building designed for The Staffordshire Bank by William Doubleday and built in 1887 was demolished, needlessly, in 1972— a great loss.

**H21 Paradise Street, The Birmingham and Midland Institute, c. 1890.**

The Birmingham and Midland Institute was founded in 1853 at the suggestion of Arthur Ryland. The new building, the foundation stone of which was laid by Prince Albert in 1855, was opened on 13th October, 1857. The design won a competition for the architect E. M. Barry, the 24 year-old son of Sir Charles Barry, and its character shows the influence of his father's later work. The Free Libraries Committee obtained Barry's services for their proposed adjoining library, but his plans were too expensive. Further plans were invited 'affording all the required accommodation with an elevation uniform with that of the Institute'. The design of William Martin and John Henry Chamberlain was accepted and the full length of Barry's elevation completed in 1865, though the portico with its naturalistic stone carving is more the work of Chamberlain. The Institute was the nineteenth century pioneer of adult education, particularly in the form of evening classes, with two departments—the Industrial and the General. Lack of space, especially in the Industrial Department, necessitated an extension. The fearless Gothic building on the left was constructed in 1878-81 to the design of John Henry Chamberlain. The Sicilian marble statue of James Watt is by Alexander Munro and was unveiled on 2nd October, 1868.

**H697 Paradise Street, Site of The Birmingham and Midland Institute, 1971.**

The Institute was demolished in 1965 to make way for the Paradise Circus development, a group of civic and cultural buildings designed by The John Madin Design Group incorporating the new Birmingham Central Library in the background and the School of Music, under construction, in the foreground. The new library is of two sections: a square inverted zigguart containing the Reference Library; and a curved wing enclosing Chamberlain Square containing the Children's Library, the Quick Reference Library and the Lending Library. The School of Music, designed to exclude noise from the adjacent road, will be over a shopping arcade. In the distance can be seen the Hall of Memory and Baskerville House dating from 1924 and 1939. The present headquarters of the Institute are at Margaret Street.

## H55 Corporation Street and Bull Street Corner, c. 1890.

The creation of Corporation Street was the main feature of Joseph Chamberlain's 1876 'Improvement Scheme' and it cut ruthlessly across the then existing Georgian street pattern. Corporation Street's 66 foot width necessitated the demolition of many old landmarks. The junction with Bull Street was opened in the 1880s, and nearly all the new properties were built on leases of seventy-five years. The miserable corner building being let by Thomas Pinson is known as Westminster Chambers. Wilkinson and Riddell's premises on the left were built in 1884, over William Jenkins' North Western Arcade on the line of the Great Western tunnel. The building on the right with the crow-stepped gables shows Flemish influence. The house on the far right is a lucky Georgian survival.

## H709 Corporation Street and Bull Street Corner, 1971.

Rackhams, a large department store founded by John Rackham who started work at Wilkinson and Riddell in 1861, was built in 1957-61 to the design of T. P. Bennett and Son. The development, which also contains individual shops and an office block known as Windsor House, is inconsistent and unconvincing as architecture, though the plan may work well. The department store is expressed separately, with zig-zag curtain walling giving the appearance of having been folded back at first floor level to reveal larger windows. Windsor House contains offices; but why has this a cornice when the department store has not? The lower floors contain a service car park but this has been expressed as offices beneath the office block and there is an awkward junction at the change in treatment. The North Western Arcade still threads its way through the site.

**H2 Jesse Collings, c. 1890.**
Jesse Collins was born in 1831 in
Devonshire, the son of a bricklayer.
He came to Birmingham as a junior clerk
to the mercantile firm of Samuel Booth
and Co. and when Booth retired in 1864
took over the business. He had been
interested in social problems before he
came to Birmingham and founded an
industrial school in Exeter. He became
secretary of the Birmingham Education
Society and then of the National Education
League. In 1868 he became a member of
the Borough Council and in 1878 Mayor.
In 1880 he entered Parliament as a Liberal
and in Gladstone's Ministry of 1886 was
appointed Parliamentary Secretary of the
Local Government Board. Collings
supported Chamberlain in his opposition to
Gladstone's policy of home rule for Ireland
and became a Unionist. From 1895-1902 he
was Under Secretary of the Home Office in
the Conservative Government. Among his
main achievements were free education,
free libraries and an art gallery for
Birmingham. He died in 1920 at Edgbaston.

## H299 The Bull Ring, St. Martin's Church, c. 1890.

The Bull Ring was once Birmingham's village green and the original parish church of Birmingham has always been on the south side of this, in the centre of the market area. The original 11th century church was rebuilt in the late 13th century and enlarged in late mediaeval times. Here are preserved the effigies of the ancient Lords of the Manor—de Bermingham.

After being encased in brick in 1690, the tower and spire were restored 1853-5 by P. C. Hardwick, and the body of the church was demolished and rebuilt 1872-5 to the design of J. A. Chatwin. The south transept window is an excellent example of the work of Birmingham's greatest painter, Sir Edward Burne Jones. The window was made 1875-80 by William Morris. The building behind the church is St. Martin's Hotel designed by Osborn and Reading.

**42 The Bull Ring, St. Martin's Church, 1971.**

In 1941 the west front of St. Martin's Church was bombed but restored in 1957, and a parish hall added by P. B. Chatwin. The concrete bridge is part of the inner ring road built 1967-71 and now known as Queensway. During the construction of the ring road, the fine Doric Market Hall 1825-8, by Charles Edge, was demolished, unnecessarily, and the bronze statue of Nelson 1807-9, the masterpiece of Sir Richard Westmancott, was shorn of its original lamp standards and sculptured reliefs around the plinth, and banished to a remote upper terrace. The concrete bridge is an ugly intrusion. Cars and walkers have been uncomfortably segregated; traffic still comes to a standstill at the top of the hill and pedestrians are subbed away through dreary underpasses.

## H15 Chamberlain Square, 1892.

To commemorate the public services of the Rt. Hon. Joseph Chamberlain to the municipality, a 'squalid area of waste land' at the back of the Town Hall was converted in 1880, by the erection of a Memorial Fountain, into 'one of the most picturesque open spaces in the town'. The square was modelled on an Italian piazza, associating local government with the Venetian city state, but the fountain, a gabled tower and spire of Portland stone, is in the 13th century French Gothic style. There is, however, some Italian inspired gold mosaic within the tracery in addition to a portrait medallion by the Pre-Raphaelite sculptor, Thomas Woolner. It was designed by John Henry Chamberlain (no relation to Joseph) who was to design the School of Art. In 1881 a statue of George Dawson, also by Woolner, was erected beneath a Gothic canopy, also by J. H. Chamberlain, but was replaced in 1884 by another statue by F. J. Williamson as the first was considered 'unsatisfactory as a work of art'. George Dawson, a local preacher, helped to found the Public Library. The Art Gallery was built in 1884-5 to the design of H. R. Yeoville Thomason as an extension to his Council House of 1874-9. The Art Gallery with its impressive full-height porch, was built over the offices of the Municipal Gas Company whose profits largely paid for the Gallery which was opened by H.R.H. The Prince of Wales on the 28th November, 1885. The red brick and terra-cotta Gothic palace on the left, also built in 1885 and originally the Liberal Club, was well designed by the local architect, Jethro A. Cossins, and shows the influence of the work of Alfred Waterhouse.

## H701 Chamberlain Square, 1971.

The Council House extension was built in 1910-19 to the sober competition-winning design of Ashley and Newman, and connected to the Art Gallery by a dramatic single-span bridge over Edmund Street. The smaller canopy and the statue of Dawson were unnecessarily removed by the Corporation in 1951. The Liberal Club was demolished in 1965. At present the whole square is being remodelled for pedestrian use as part of the new Birmingham Central Library complex designed by The John Madin Design Group.

## H40 Colmore Row from the Town Hall, c. 1898.

This end of Colmore Row was originally Ann Street and cut diagonally across what is now Victoria Square. Ann Street contained red brick Georgian houses but was not entirely built-up in 1825, when the right-hand side was rebuilt with elegant terrace houses faced with stucco. The left-hand side, which is part of the New Hall Colmore Estate, was not rebuilt until after 1866 when the leases began to fall in. The Colmore family insisted on a common roofline and the 'grand manner'. Colmore Row was widened in accordance with Ann Street to which it gave its name. The widening, completed in 1874, resulted in a continuous line of stone-faced Italian palaces from the Great Western Hotel to the Council House. Lloyds Bank, next to the Council House, was completed in 1871 to the design of J. A. Chatwin and led to the creation of Eden Place. Christ Church, usually called the Free Church because there was no charge for 1300 of its 1800 sittings, was erected from 1805 to 1813, the spire and portico being added in 1815. The church as built, unfairly described by Longford as 'certainly one of the ugliest in the town', differs considerably from the original design by Charles Norton, which showed a dome on the top of the tower similar to that of St. Philip's. John Baskerville (1706-75), the famous Birmingham printer, was buried in the vaults. On 12th April, 1893 a leaden coffin was found to which were soldered letters in metal type forming his name. In the coffin was found a knife for spreading printers' ink.

## H696 Colmore Row from the Town Hall, 1971.

Christ Church was demolished in 1899 and replaced by Christ Church Buildings (popularly known as Galloways' Corner), which were taken down in 1970. The site is to be paved as part of Victoria Square so the new views of the Town Hall and Council House will fortunately be retained. Lloyds Bank and the adjoining building were rebuilt in 1962-3 as a new regional head office for Lloyds—a flat design by Easton, Robertson, Cusdin, Preston and Smith.

**H64 New Street from the Town Hall, c. 1895.**

New Street dates from the early 14th century. The statue in the foreground is of Sir Robert Peel by Peter Hollins and was unveiled on 27th August, 1855. In 1842 Peel granted Birmingham's first measure of self-government. Peter Hollins was the son of a sculptor, Williams Hollins (1763-1843), who was the leading local architect at the beginning of the 19th century. On the left is Christ Church, opened in 1813, and further down the same side is the portico of the building completed in 1829 for the Birmingham Society of Arts. The General Post Office on the right, designed by Sir H. Tanner and opened in December 1890, was described in *The Builder* for that year as "coarse and commonplace in architectural design. Pots and tean-urns of abnormal dimensions are perched about on ledges and on cornices; the whole of it is fussy, pretentious, and totally wanting in dignity or breadth of effect—it is difficult to understand the production of anything so ostentatiously bad as this. Has it been the result of a kind of 'spirituel' attempt to harmonise with the environment?" This is harsh criticism. We now see the General Post Office as a French chateau, in natural stone, with an intricate roof-line of pavilions and chimneys set against steeply sloping slate roofs—a picturesque building that would contrast well with the machine-finished structures of today. The horse bus is waiting to pick up passengers for Five Ways. This remarkable photograph by Thomas Lewis was taken on a 12-inch by 10-inch glass plate.

**599 New Street from the Town Hall, 1971.**

Christ Church was demolished in 1899 and replaced by Christ Church Buildings—a large six-storey block of offices in the Flemish Renaissance style (generally known as Galloways' Corner). This was designed by Essex, Nicol and Goodman, and as it followed the line of the footpath its construction considerably reduced the apparent size of the square. It was demolished in 1970 and the site is to be paved as part of Victoria Square. Waterloo House, which replaced Waterloo Bar Buildings in 1926, was also designed by Essex and Goodman, but in a thin clasical style. The well-proportioned elevations, faced with cream faience, are being cleaned following the demolition of Christ Church Buildings. Rowans has an interesting modernistic interior designed by P. J. Westwood in the 1930s but his black shop-front has unfortunately been painted white. The G.P.O. Building awaits its fate. Planning permission for a 280 ft. 'sculptured' office block on the site has been refused by the City Council. Such a tower block would be out of scale in Victoria Square.

**H65 New Street from High Street, c. 1895.**

Albion House on the left, occupied by Turner Son and Nephew, drapers, is an interesting commercial building in the classical style with cast-iron framing to the shops and first-floor display windows. Next to this is Lloyds Bank, formerly the Birmingham Joint Stock Bank Limited, a dignified classical design in the grand manner by F. B. Osborn in 1875. Then a gap, the site of the Hen and Chickens of 1798 probably designed by James Wyatt. Later this was filled by the Hen and Chickens Hotel designed for the Birmingham Coffee House Company Limited by the local architect, J. A. Chatwin (a pupil of Barry), in the Gothic style in deference to the adjoining King Edward VI High School for Boys. The hotel was, however, to be of red terra-cotta though the school is of Darley Dale sandstone. The Free Grammar School, founded in 1552, was rebuilt in 1833-37 to the design of Charles Barry and Augustus Welby Pugin following an open competition. Their building, the first scholarly secular Gothic-revival building in the town, pre-dates the work of these architects at the Palace of Westminster, London. Beyond (above the policeman's head) is J. A. Chatwin's first Gothic building in New Street—the 1877 extension of Exchange Buildings. This is followed by the parent Exchange Buildings (1863-5), designed by Edward Holmes, carrying a slender corner spire. In the distance is Christ Church and on the right the beginning of the recently cut Corporation Street. Not a car in sight though Wolseley were producing a three-wheeler with a 2 h.p. engine.

**675 New Street from High Street, 1971.**

Lloyds Bank was rebuilt up to the corner of Worcester Street in 1919 to the designs of P. B. Chatwin and demolished in 1971 revealing the side of the Hen and Chickens Hotel now known as the Arden Hotel. The bank was transferred to the Rotunda on the left, built in 1965 to the design of James A. Roberts, and to be extended over the old bank site. King Edward's was transferred to Edgbaston in 1936 and replaced by the Odeon cinema and a sober Portland stone block in the classical style by Essex, Nicol and Goodman. The Exchange was demolished in 1965 to make way for a clinical slab of offices by Cotton, Ballard and Blow, now occupied by the Midland Bank, who have deserted their fine palazzo which now stands empty on the other side of Stephenson Place. This palazzo was built in 1867-9 to the design of Edward Holmes, and is just visible above the podium of the new Midland Bank. Christ Church was demolished in 1899. The building on the right of the picture is City Centre House—shops and offices of little architectural merit built in 1955-61 to the design of Cotton, Ballard and Blow on a three-acre site following extensive destruction by bombs during World War II. It has arcades as before and is serviced from below ground under High Street.

**H67 New Street, Moore's Oyster Rooms, c. 1898.**

Arthur Moore opened his Oyster Rooms below Christ Church in 1881 and carried on his business there for almost twenty years, after which he moved to Cannon Street. When the cellars were demolished about 1899 seaweed was found growing from the walls! This picture by Thomas Lewis includes, on the right-hand side, a showcase of his photographs.

**H704 New Street, Site of Moore's Oyster Rooms, 1972.**

Galloways' Corner, which replaced Christ Church, was demolished in 1970 and the site will be paved as part of Victoria Square. The buildings between Colmore Row and Waterloo Street were to have been demolished to make way for a widened Colmore Row in connection with the inner-ring road scheme, with an open space from the Town Hall to Birmingham Cathedral. However, after pressure from local amenity societies, the Council decided not to go ahead with its plans. To have encouraged traffic through this area would have been a grave mistake; besides the demolition of individual buildings of merit a characterful area would have been lost, including the separate identities of Victoria Square and St. Philip's Churchyard. The area has now been designated a conservation area and is being given new life. The building (with the clock) in the style of Sir Christopher Wren was constructed in 1904 for the Alliance Assurance Company. **Right:** Enlarged detail of H67.

**H7 New Street Railway Station, c. 1900**
This station and Queen's Hotel designed by William Livlock were built in 1854 and shared by both the London and North Western Railway and the Midland Railway. They are in a restrained Barryesque Tuscan Doric style with the tracks and platforms covered by a curved roof, supported on 36 single-span trussed cast-iron arches, each weighing 25 tons. The bridge over the tracks and a central carriage drive known as Queen's Drive is a public right-of-way from the booking hall in Stephenson Place to Station Street. In 1880 the station was doubled in size to occupy $14\frac{1}{2}$ acres.

**670 New Street Railway Station, 1971.**
1945 bomb damage occurred and it was
ecided to take down the roof structure.
ebuilding started in 1964 as part of the
ondon Midland Region's modernisation
nd electrification plan. The new station,
esigned by the British Railways Architects
epartment, has 12 platforms covered by a
ven-acre concrete slab and connected by
calators and staircases to a spacious
ooking hall above. Here are the offices
and shops known as the Birmingham
Shopping Centre. These were constructed
in 1968 to the design of Cotton, Ballard
and Blow retaining the pedestrian right-of-
way to give direct access into the Bull Ring
Centre. The block of flats on the left is
Stephenson Tower designed by the City
Architect and constructed as part of a plan
to bring back life to the city centre at
night. **Overleaf.** Enlarged detail of H7.

**H35 New Street/Ethel Street,
The Colonnade Hotel, c. 1900.**
This free-standing French Renaissance
block, built in 1882 as shops and offices,
was designed by W. H. Ward (the architect
of the Great Western Arcade, 1876) and
was later converted into an arcade with
restaurants and further shops by Oliver
Essex. Essex was articled to W. H. Ward
and may have been responsible for the
design of the original building just before he
commenced practice in 1883. The upper
floors certainly lack the bold handling
expected of Ward and there are plenty of
elaborate gables which, developed in a
more Flemish form, were to become the
hallmark of Essex's work. The upper floors
are occupied by The Colonnade Hotel.

**95  New Street, Woolworth Building and Winston Churchill House, 1972.**

The Colonnade Hotel closed in 1916, Mr. C. Lancaster being the last manager. Subsequently the building became the Chamber of Commerce but was demolished with the Theatre Royal in 1961 after the new Chamber of Commerce had been built in Edgbaston. The consultant architects for the Woolworth building in New Street, which incorporates the Conservative Club

by H. Bloomer and Son, were Cotton, Ballard and Blow. It is mainly faced with brick at upper level and its bulk is most obtrusive from both Victoria Square and Navigation Street.

**H17 Victoria Square, The Council House and Art Gallery, 1901.**

The statue of Queen Victoria is a replica in Sicilian marble of the statue by Thomas Brock, in the Shire Hall, Worcester. It was offered to the Council in 1897, the year of Queen Victoria's Diamond Jubilee, by William Barber in memory of his father and was unveiled in Council House Square on the 10th January, 1901, a few days before the death of Queen Victoria.

Alderman Edwards, the Lord Mayor, undertook that the statue 'be preserved in its present position for all future time' and the square became known as Victoria Square. The other statues are of Joseph Priestley and John Skirrow Wright, both by A. W. Williamson. The statue of Joseph Priestley erected by public subscription in 1874 shows him making the experiment which led to the discovery of oxygen. The statue of John Skirrow Wright was unveiled

by John Bright on 15th June, 1883. Wright was a popular lay preacher and Liberal leader. The site for the Council House was bought by the Borough Council in 1853 with the intention of building council offices and law courts, but competitive designs for the new building were not invited until 1870. Out of the twenty-nine designs submitted the committee, which included Alfred Waterhouse, considered that of a local

architect, H. R. Yeoville Thomason, to the best. The Council House was built from 1874-9 with a row of columns in sympathy with the neighbouring Town Hall. The bold centrepiece, enclosing a mosaic by the Venice and Murano Company, supports a pediment containing a sculptured group portraying Britannia rewarding the Birmingham manufacture. The dome is disappointingly slender. The segmental pediments containing sculptur

oups representing literature, art and ience in relation to industry, herald the Idition to the borough arms in 1889 of e supporting figures 'Industry' and 'Art' r the new City of Birmingham. The horse is in the foreground, on its way from ve Ways to Snow Hill Station, is operated r the Birmingham Tramway Co. Ltd.

**H702 Victoria Square, The Council House and Art Gallery, 1971.**
In 1913 the statues of Joseph Priestley and John Skirrow Wright were moved to Chamberlain Square and replaced by a statue of Edward VII by Albert Toft.
In turn this was removed to Highgate Park and the statue of Queen Victoria, restored by William Bloye, cast in bronze and mounted on a new pedestal, was unveiled by H.R.H. Princess Elizabeth in 1951.

The Council House has lost its chimneys and original roof tiling and has been cleaned, but the carved capitals and frieze cannot be fully appreciated as they are covered with wire mesh to keep away starlings. The unsightly haunchings over the capitals are also for this purpose. On the right, the front of Lloyds Bank follows the cornice line set by the Colmore family for Colmore Row in the 1860s but does not conceal the bulk of building further back.

## H1774 The General Electric Company Limited, Witton, 1901.

In 1901 the GEC began building its 110-acre site at Witton, where at that time there were few industrial premises. 'Taking Birmingham and district as a whole, by 1911 there were over 7,000 employed in the production of dynamos, motor magnetos, pumps, meters and transformers. Birmingham also became the wireless capital of the Midlands, from the time of the first broadcast under the 5IT sign from GEC in November 1922'. But the heavy engineering side of GEC Witton contributed most to its fame if not its fortunes. Generating plant was developed for the home and overseas markets, particularly for Commonwealth countries.

## H748 The General Electric Company Limited, Witton, 1971.

After World War II there was a shortage of everything. For about fifteen years 'Reconstruction' gave the capital goods industry a blank cheque. By 1960, however, there were clear signs that there were too many heavy electrical engineering companies. The British Empire had gone; Commonwealth countries were self-sustaining or being wooed by Japan. The Central Electricity Generating Board and the Government encouraged rationalisation. AEI, English Electric and GEC subsequently merged. Over 50,000 workers became redundant. Other sections of GEC have flourished, but Birmingham's Witton has changed out of all recognition. Indeed a major employer on the site is now Parsons-Reyrolle—GEC's competitor.

### H329 High Street, from Dale End, c. 1903.

The original houses in High Street were half-timbered. The last surviving example dating from 1576, was removed as late as 1850. The roadway was used as a cattle market and as it was also the starting place for the London stage coach, High Street was very congested before it was widened. The first four buildings on the left, faced with stucco, date from about 1830 and are followed by a grand classical design with a strong over-hanging cornice, possibly of the 1870s. Next is an early Georgian house converted into a shop. On the right, behind an Edwardian post box, is a shop advertising 'Modes Parisienne' and another dress shop of the 1890s, followed by the restrained stone-faced Tuscan Doric Lloyds Bank, originally the residence of John Taylor of Taylor and Lloyds, founded in Dale End in 1765. High Street was Lloyds' head offices from 1815-1871 when a new head office was built in Colmore Row. Beyond Union Street is an interesting iron-clad building with curved corner windows.

### H747 High Street from Dale End, 1971.

The building on the left possibly dates from the 1860s when this end of High Street was widened. The road in the foregound is over the tunnel of the Great Western Railway and the warehouses on this side of Carr's Lane, on the left, are carried on cantilevers over this tunnel. Marks & Spencer, built in the mid-1950s with classical touches, makes no attempt to recognise the Modern Movement but the Co-operative has a streamlined shiny black granite and glass extension built in the 1930s. The nondescript buildings on the right are serviced from the ring road by means of a tunnel under the road.
The Rotunda, built in 1964-5, is one of Birmingham's most prominent landmarks. It is well sited on high ground above the Bull Ring and its definite shape contrasts well with the surrounding jumble of buildings. The proportions of the block however, are too squat and could have been considerably improved by glazing the spandrels to reduce the striped effect.
The building in the distance is the Bull Ring Centre, built 1961-4.

**H331 The Old Square, c. 1903.**

Prior to the construction of Corporation Street, Old Square was a quiet space surrounded by an important group of early Georgian houses. In this photograph, the store on the left, built in 1883 to the design of Kirk and Jones, is occupied by Jevons and Mellors, gentlemen's hosiers, and has a service drive from Old Square beneath the dome. Newbury's Limited was built in 1896. Charles Newbury was responsible in his youth for advertising Hudson's Dry Soap and later turned his goods warehouse in Old Square into 'a great bargain emporium'. The building, designed by the vigorous firm of architects, Essex, Nicol and Goodman, is an interesting structure in red terra-cotta with large areas of window on the lower floors. This requirement probably determined the choice of material which, because of its hard shiny surface, looks more satisfactory in slender sections than stone. The curved walls of the building certainly express this hard shiny surface, though the central feature is not in sympathy with their undulating effect. The terra-cotta building on the right was also designed by Essex, Nicol and Goodman, this time for Lunt and Company. The steam trams—these are bound for Perry Barr—were replaced by electric trams in 1906.

**H723 The Old Square, 1971.**

In 1885 Lewis's was opened on the corner of Corporation Street and Bull Street but by the 1920s the building was found inadequate and demolished together with Jevons and Mellors' building. A new building extending from Bull Street to Old square was erected to the design of G. de C. Fraser and a few years later another block of similar design was erected on the site of Newbury's which had been acquired in 1926 to prevent further competition from this 'great bargain emporium'. Both buildings are of stone, in a severe classical style and linked by two bridges across the Minories supported on free-standing Tuscan Doric columns near to the kerb. There are also subways and in 1971 floors were constructed between the bridges so the Minories is now a continuous covered arcade. On the right Bell, Nicolson and Lunt, wholesale drapers and warehousemen, have also rebuilt their premises.

**H330 Bull Street, from High Street, c. 1910.**

Bull Street, the site of the mediaeval priory and church and formerly known as Chappell Street, owes its present name to the 16th century Bull Inn. In 1824 John Cadbury set up a shop in Bull Street. Although he sold tea and other goods, cocoa became the most important article of his trade and, when he moved, the business of tea-dealer was handed on to his nephew and developed into Barrow's Stores, on the extreme left. Southalls, on the right, was opened in 1820 by Thomas Southall who was joined by his brother William, and this venture developed into the well-known firm of manufacturing chemists. The charming Gothic shop-front dates from the second-half of the 19th century. The next shop on the right is Dunn's advertising hats, followed by the Falstaff, and then Dean's advertising carpets and linoleum. Dean's, built on the corner of Corporation Street in 1886, has two gold domes and was designed by the architect of the North Western Arcade, William Jenkins, who took his inspiration from Lewis's new building. Lewis's, designed by H. R. Yeoville Thomason, was opened in 1885 and there were 40,000 visitors on the first day. Joseph Chamberlain himself is reputed to have induced Lewis to take this corner site.

**H734 Bull Street from High Street, 1971.**

Lewis's and Newbury's were rebuilt in the 1920s as Lewis's new premises. These are linked directly to a pedestrian shopping area beneath the intersection of Corporation Street and Bull Street. In 1963-5 Dean's and the adjoining buildings were replaced by Colonnade Developments designed by Frederick Gibberd, and Barrow's moved across the road. The arcade links a central pedestrian area on the right known as Corporation Square to another pedestrian area on the other side of Bull Street known as Martineau Square in the Corporation Street Estate Company Building. The architects for this development, which replaced the original Barrow's Stores in the late 1960s, were J. Seymour Harris and Partners, and it is faced with their favourite white marble. Beyond, is Windsor House, designed by T. P. Bennett and Son, part of the 1957-61 development by Rackham's Stores. The upper part of Bull Street, which has been planted with trees, is to become part of a new pedestrian way from Old Square to Cherry Street and will become a bus-only road.

**H542 Wolseley Racing Car, c. 1905.**
This 96 h.p. chain driven Wolseley was raced by the Hon. C. S. Rolls in the 60-mile Gordon-Bennett Trials at Auvergn, France on 5th July, 1905. The Wolseley won, 47 seconds ahead of a Napier. Frederick York Wolseley was born in 1837. In 1867 he went out to Australia to manage a farm and shear sheep by hand. The experience turned him into an engineer. He was joined by Herbert Austin who had emigrated to Australia as a youth. In 1899 Wolseley came back to England. He brought with him a new company—The Wolseley Sheep Shearing Machine Company Limited—the forerunner of the famous Birmingham motor car industry. Wolseley died in 1899. The building in the background is St. Peter's College, College Walk, Saltley. **Left:** Enlarged detail of H542.

**H334 New Street, from Worcester Street, c. 1910.**

New Street dates from the 14th century when it started at the village High Street and ended in the country. Between Cannon Street and Corporation Street are the stone-faced offices of The Birmingham Daily Post with classical semi-circular arched windows and strong cornices. They were designed by H. R. Yeoville Thomason and extended by him into Cannon Street in 1884. The other corner against Corporation Street, known as Queen's Corner, was built in accordance with Thomason's cornice heights when Corporation Street was cut. On this side of Corporation Street is another stone-faced classical building known as Prince's Corner, designed by A. Edward Dempster and R. A. Heaton. Next to this is Warwick House, an elegant four storey building in the classical style, designed by W. Thomas for William Holliday in 1839 and later doubled in width towards High Street. The next building, Hyam and Co., is considerably taller and in a French Renaissance style. The symmetrical building in the foreground, over the Midland Arcade, is a jolly Art Nouveau interpretation of classical themes in terra-cotta by T. W. F. Newton and Cheatle whose short-lived practice set a high standard of design at the turn of the century and considerably influenced the development of the New Hall Colmore Estate. The shop on the corner of the Arcade is H. J. Whitlock, photographer, who took the picture.

**H736 New Street, from Worcester Street, 1971.**

In 1965 The Birmingham Post and Mail moved to Colmore Circus and their buildings have since been carefully restored and converted into shops by Cotton, Ballard and Blow. Warwick House was demolished before the last war and work commenced on the construction of a new Warwick House, for Marshall and Snelgrove. The unfinished building suffered bomb damage during the war but was subsequently completed. Marshall and Snelgrove closed their Birmingham store in 1970 and Warwick House is now being converted into an hotel. City Centre House on the right, by Cotton, Ballard and Blow, was built in 1955-6 and incorporates the Midland Arcade following the destruction of the previous building by enemy action.

**H30 New Street, Royal Birmingham Society of Artists, 1912.**
This building, designed by Thomas Rickman and Henry Hutchinson, was completed in 1829. Rickman was a Gothic scholar 'who first correctly named the several styles and clearly elucidated the principles of our ecclesiastical architecture', but Hutchinson, who was a member of the Academy of Arts from which the Society grew, was a classical architect and the building is generally considered to be his work. The handsome exterior is well proportioned and faultlessly detailed. Originally there were no windows, the central door leading to a sequence of elegant top-lit rooms obviously influenced in form by the work of Sir John Soane at the Bank of England, London.

**H703 New Street, Royal Birmingham Society of Artists, 1971.**
Due to failing visits by the public and increasing costs the Society was forced to leave its galleries in 1911 and Hutchinson's building was demolished to make way for New Street Chambers, a very poor block of shops and offices in the classical style faced with cream faience. The Society secured a 100 year lease of a specially designed gallery above the new shops but it is a pity that they did not insist on an excellent design for the new building. The demolition of the old building could have been prevented today though we still pull down buildings of quality.

## H591 Paradise Street, The Town Hall, 1913.

In 1830 the design of J. A. Hansom and E. Welch won the open competition for a Town Hall. Construction began in 1832 but by 1834 the architects, who had to stand surety for the building, were declared bankrupt. The local architect, Charles Edge, who had designed the Market Hall, was appointed supervising architect and added two bays to accommodate the organ. The building was opened before its completion for the Musical Festival of 1834. Mendelssohn's *Elijah* and Elgar's *Dream of Gerontius* were first performed here. It is a copy in Anglesey marble of the Temple of Castor and Pollux in the Roman Forum, set on a battered rusticated base. The building is fresh and impressive, though the limestone has weathered. The superb silhouette of the former Liberal Club occupied by the Norwich Union can be fully appreciated from this viewpoint.

## H737 Paradise Street, The Town Hall, 1971.

The Town Hall has been cleaned and re-roofed. The Birmingham and Midland Institute and the Liberal Club have both been demolished to make way for Paradise Circus. On the left, Richard Seifert's Paradise Centre for A.T.V. is under construction. Seen end-on from the Civic Centre this slender block of offices is surprisingly dramatic and contrasts well with the surrounding buildings, but from Colmore Row it is an unwelcome backcloth to the Town Hall.

## H589 Corporation Street, from New Street, 1920.

'The Builder' for 1st November 1890, states that "taking the average architecture of the town as exhibited in Corporation Street, which is the costliest street in Birmingham in this respect, the impression left on the mind is quite painful, the more so from the amount of display and the show of lavish expenditure in making buildings 'ornamental' which is to be seen everywhere". Most of the buildings, which vary in quality, were designed by local architects in either the Gothic or Renaissance styles. Queen's Corner on the left is a continuation of The Birmingham Daily Post (see page 82). Next to Queen's Corner is Victoria Buildings, a French Renaissance design with rounded bay windows, then a classical building with Gothic bay windows, followed by Central Chambers of 1880 by W. H. Ward, and Fletcher's Chambers of 1888 by Osborn and Reading. On the far corner of Fore Street is Pattison's, a poor Gothic design of 1887 by Dempster and Heaton. The most outstanding building to be seen at this end of the street is the Cobden Hotel, a spiky Gothic fantasy in stone with a slender spire, designed by William Doubleday for The Birmingham Coffee House Company Limited and opened by John Bright in 1883. Lewis's domed corner building was opened in 1885 and the Central Hall in the distance in 1904.

## H732 Corporation Street, from New Street, 1971.

Pattison's, which has lost its spire, went out of business in the 1960s. The Cobden Hotel was demolished in 1958 to make way for Rackhams. Lewis's was rebuilt in the 1920s. On the right, C & A was rebuilt after World War II and as the new building is set back, the Victoria Temperance Hotel, lately the New Victoria Hotel, can now be seen. This restrained dignified structure was built in 1887 with giant pilasters rising through three storeys.

**H615 Five Ways, 1920.**
This was Birmingham's boundary in 1807.
In 1813 oil lighting was provided for
Broad Street for seven months of the year
and until 1840 tolls were taken at Five
Ways for the upkeep of the highway.
By 1920 this end of Broad Street consists
mainly of Georgian houses, either converted
into shops or with shops built on the front
gardens. The construction of these shops
must have considerably reduced the

apparent width of the street, but the
avenue of plane trees softens the effect of
commerce. The white marble statue of
Joseph Sturge, a pioneer of adult
education, is by John Thomas and dates
from 1862. Thomas had executed all the
ornamental and carved stone and
woodwork at the Grammar School in
New Street—a task which took him three
years to complete—and was engaged by
Charles Barry to superintend the stone-

rving of the entire Palace of Westminster, ndon. This statue of Sturge is one of his t works and was unfinished at the time his death. The red terra-cotta building the left, possibly designed by Osborn d Reading, is a branch of the Midland nk. The white Portland stone classical ilding on the right is a branch of Lloyds nk built in 1908-9 to the design of B. Chatwin.

**H754 Five Ways, 1971.**
The human scale and charm of the nineteenth century have been ruthlessly swept away to provide an elevated round-about of roads above a central area of paving linked to the scattered offices and shopping centres. The central pedestrian area has been designed to receive a restaurant. Auchinleck House, on the right, was constructed in 1964. Primarily it is a shopping centre with a rather draughty

pedestrian precinct. Loading and unloading facilities on the first-floor are gained by way of a ramp. Above is an eleven-storey office block, placed unforgivably on the diagonal of the two mains roads so that it is out of line with all the surrounding buildings. The end facing Five Ways has been splayed and provided with two meaningless mosaic murals. **Overleaf** Enlarged detail of H615.

COMPLETE FOOD

CONTAINS FRUIT

HARVO

NOURISHMENT

EXTREME DIGESTIBILITY

SOLE MANUFACTURERS R.WINTER LTD

SOLD BY ALL BAKERS GROCERS ETC

RICHLY MALTED CAKE

NESTLE'S

SWISS

MILK

The Richest in Cream.

O·9914

USED TICKETS

"RAIN COATS"

CAMETA RUBBER CO

93 JOHN BRIGHT ST B'HAM

WATER PROOFS

CAMETA RUBBER CO

93 JOHN BRIGHT ST B'HAM

**513 Colmore Row, Snow Hill tation, 1926.**

he station was opened in 1854 and by 79 was handling 200 trains a day. he Great Western Hotel was added in 63 to the design of J. A. Chatwin and the tion behind rebuilt from 1871-1912 ring which time the passenger entrance as broken through the hotel to continue e line of Great Western Arcade (1875-6) posite. The hotel shows the influence of

Sir Charles Barry, to whom Chatwin was articled, notably the attic storeys of the end pavilions and their corner chimneys. The general composition is strong and vigorous and the detail impeccable, especially on the return elevation to Snow Hill, with very little carved decoration other than mouldings. Colmore Row was the terminus for trams from the north-west, including services 24 and 25 from Lozells which were replaced by buses in 1950.

**H735 Colmore Row, Snow Hill, 1971.**
The Great Western Hotel, simply planned, with wide corridors and airy rooms, could easily have been converted to another use. It was torn down in 1970 to make way for offices. Will these new offices be as attractive as Chatwin's hotel? This is certainly possible—provided the developer of this major Birmingham site makes a determined effort to ensure that it will be so.

# Summary 1857–1972

by Douglas Hickman

The old photographs give an indication of how Birmingham changed from an industrial Georgian town to a commercial Victorian city. Some mediaeval half-timbered buildings survived well into the 19th century and combined with neglected Georgian houses, presented a very Dickensian scene.

Twice in just over one hundred years the centre of Birmingham has been rebuilt on the main lines of its original plan. The Georgian town was rebuilt by the Victorians and now their city is rapidly being replaced.

The elimination of the Georgian scene started with the introduction of the railways into the heart of the town, necessitating widespread demolition and producing the Queen's Hotel of 1854 and the Great Western Hotel of 1863 both in a grand Italianate style. These set the scale for subsequent redevelopment especially the rebuilding between 1863 and 1873 of the whole of the north side of Colmore Row from Snow Hill to the Council House in a straight line and to a set cornice height resulting in an impressive unified sequence of stone faced classical facades.

Two years later Joseph Chamberlain launched his Improvement Scheme, which condemned the central slums and the inadequacy of the existing road system and proposed a plan to drive a new street 'as broad as a Parisian boulevard' through the unhealthy areas. No doubt Chamberlain was impressed by Colmore Row and had in mind Haussmann's long wide straight roads cut through the centre of Paris for the sake of civic pride. The plan shows the new street (now Corporation Street) cutting ruthlessly across the Georgian street pattern from New Street to the Aston Road (as shown on the 1875 map on page seventeen) but bent around Old Square, the finest Georgian square in the town. It came so close to Old Square however that this was later opened into the street and entirely rebuilt.

Corporation Street cleared away the slums and opened up the centre of the town but fell far short of Chamberlain's dream of a Parisian boulevard. Visually it was a disaster; it had been compromised by being curved and neither end had a large scale building to terminate the vista. Martin and Chamberlain, the architects and surveyors for the scheme, were not classicists and shattered the concept of a grand formal thoroughfare by constructing the first building, on the corner of Warwick Passage, in their favourite picturesque Venetian Gothic style with gables, for John Henry Chamberlain (no relation to Joseph) was a student and disciple of Ruskin. A battle of the styles followed and was not quelled till 1887, when Sir Aston Webb and Ingress Bell won the competition for the Victoria Law Courts with a vigorous design in the French Renaissance style of Francis I in bright red terracotta. This building so influenced subsequent developments that the northern end of the street acquired a distinct character of its own which is still impressive.

As a shopping street however Corporation Street was a success combined with the many covered arcades which became such an important feature of the town centre. Shops were serviced from the old roads at the rear leaving the thoroughfare clear, though many of the articles bought would have been delivered rather than taken away by individuals.

The next major planning scheme was for a new Civic Centre; this was designed in 1935 but at the outbreak of war in 1939 only two thirds of the first block (now known as Baskerville House) had been completed and the scheme was later abandoned in favour of a freer arrangement.

By 1943 the congestion of traffic in the city centre required major road improvements so they city council decided to construct a ring road round the central shopping area, picking up the radial roads at large islands. This was designed by the City Engineer, Sir Herbert Manzoni and its construction from 1967-1971 swept away many old buildings. In places, such as the Bull Ring, the new road is most obstrusive especially where it is not bounded by buildings but where it comes near to the civic buildings it disappears underground and avoids any intrusion.

During the construction of the ring road, new department stores, shops and offices were built in both New Street and Corporation Street but these were uninspired. They missed the opportunity of contrasting modern lightweight materials and clear-cut forms with the solid masonry and elaborate silhouettes of the previous century.

At the same time five areas around the city centre were completely rebuilt resulting in a forest of tower blocks of flats which, though not as satisfactory as houses and gardens for family life, have given a sense of space and are an impressive sight from some approaches to the city, notably the Belgrave Road.

Having completed the new ring road, now known as Queensway, the city council is turning its attention to the improvement of the area within; Victoria Square has been enlarged and with St. Philip's Churchyard and the interesting group of buildings in-between these two open spaces have been designated a conservation area. Chamberlain Place is being re-modelled around the Chamberlain Memorial and the new Central Library will frame some impressive views of the older buildings. Plans are being prepared to eliminate motor traffic from many shopping streets so at last the pedestrian, who is forced to go underground whenever he encounters a major road, is likely to be allowed to walk and shop again without interruption.

Will the city continue to be rebuilt on such a scale? Rebuilding is necessary to enable a city to flourish but the increasing awareness of the scenic value of certain older buildings and the creation of conservation areas will prevent widespread demolition in parts of the city centre and other areas where there are concentrations of well designed older buildings. These should not however become museum pieces, but be allowed to evolve to meet the needs of the day, with honest modern redevelopments in scale with the existing surroundings resulting in a rich environment consisting of the best of all periods.

There are of course large areas of the city completely devoid of individual buildings of merit, or of buildings which have any value as a group, which call for comprehensive redevelopment, and these are likely to be rebuilt on a large scale. Many areas, however, have well built 19th century terrace houses, the best of which should be imaginatively converted for modern use to retain some of the history and identity of a place after it has been redeveloped. Birmingham people are used to changing surroundings but are human enough to want the old landmarks which give them a sense of belonging.

**Overleaf:** H946 Birmingham's city centre seen from The Sentinels flats, 1971.

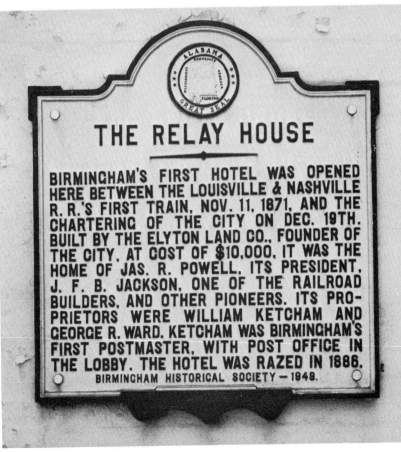

## THE RELAY HOUSE

BIRMINGHAM'S FIRST HOTEL WAS OPENED
HERE BETWEEN THE LOUISVILLE & NASHVILLE
R. R.'S FIRST TRAIN, NOV. 11, 1871, AND THE
CHARTERING OF THE CITY ON DEC. 19TH.
BUILT BY THE ELYTON LAND CO., FOUNDER OF
THE CITY, AT COST OF $10,000, IT WAS THE
HOME OF JAS. R. POWELL, ITS PRESIDENT,
J. F. B. JACKSON, ONE OF THE RAILROAD
BUILDERS, AND OTHER PIONEERS. ITS PRO-
PRIETORS WERE WILLIAM KETCHAM AND
GEORGE R. WARD. KETCHAM WAS BIRMINGHAM'S
FIRST POSTMASTER, WITH POST OFFICE IN
THE LOBBY. THE HOTEL WAS RAZED IN 1886.
BIRMINGHAM HISTORICAL SOCIETY — 1949.

# Birmingham, Alabama, 1972

by John Whybrow

**City of Birmingham,
Office of the Mayor,
City Hall,
Birmingham,
Alabama.**

It is with real pleasure, during our
centennial year, that I send warm
greetings on behalf of the City of
Birmingham, Alabama to the Lord
Mayor, the Council and Citizens of
Birmingham, England.

Mr. John Whybrow's report of his
visit to our city was first published
in your own *Birmingham Post*
on 10th June, 1972. We thought so
highly of this article that I arranged
for copies to be sent to civic leaders
in Birmingham, in Alabama, and
all over the United States. I am
particularly glad, therefore, that the
account now appears in permanent
form so that it may continue to
strengthen the bond of friendship
between our two cities and countries.

George G. Seibels, Jr.,
Mayor

**Left:** H902 Birmingham, Alabama seen from the ridge of Jones Valley. The valley was probably a no man's land between the Indian Cherokees, Chicksaws, Creeks and Choctaws. In 1815 Samuel Fields, Isaac Fields, Andrew McLaughlin and John Jones, the first white pioneers, created a settlement and built a log fort. David Crockett, the famous frontiersman, visited Jones Valley in 1818 and later recommended other settlers to come down from Tennessee. Townships and villages sprang up during the next 45 years including Elyton, which became the county town of Jefferson. In 1871 the railroads, one from Chattanooga in the north and the other from Montgomery in the south, crossed two miles beyond Elyton at the centre of an unborn city—Birmingham.

H91 The plaque outside the railway station commemorates The Relay House, Birmingham's first hotel. There were mosquito nets for the beds but few luxuries. However, The Relay House was the centre of Birmingham's social life in the early days as well as the waiting room for railway passengers. The hotel, subsequently taken down to make way for a new station, was in 1882 one of the original subscribers to the Bell Telephone Company's first exchange in Birmingham. Initially the Bell representative had difficulty finding twenty-five subscribers, the minimum number to justify an installation.

H923 The Bell Telephone Company's new building in Nineteenth Street North, which administers operations in Alabama and surrounding states. In front is the First United Methodist Church. The land was given by the Elyton Land Company which founded Birmingham; they also gave land to the Presbyterians, Episcopalians, Catholics, Baptists, Cumberland Presbyterians and Jews. The De Soto rooms refer to the Spanish explorer Hernando de Soto who crossed Alabama in 1541. Indians almost wiped out the expedition.

**Right:** H992 The new 30-storey headquarters of The First National Bank of Birmingham, clad with reflective glass, contains 450,000 sq. ft. of office space plus parking for 390 cars in the square building in front. The bank, founded in 1873 by Charles Linn, was Birmingham's first brick building, three storeys high and nicknamed Linn's Folly. On the left, the Federal Building U.S. Courthouse.

The truck driver next to me at the coffee bar asked: 'What do you
[wa]nt to come here for?'

He was pleased – and curious. He could have understood a tourist
[go]ing to, say, New York or Miami, but why Birmingham, Alabama?

I explained that I came in peace and that I was from Birmingham,
[ne]ar Stratford-upon-Avon, England. I gave further details. I had come,
[I] said, to gather information on the origins and growth of Birmingham,
[Al]abama, for a book I was editing. I was also hoping to finance my trip
[wi]th pre-sales of the book.

His opinion of me took a sharp upwards turn. He approved of this
[m]otive. In America selling is as honourable as buying. From that moment
[w]e got along fine.

I had other reasons, too. For example, my business had been
[fo]unded the same year as his Birmingham. That is in 1871. And as
[re]gards Alabama and the other States of the South, Churchill had written
[of] the closing stages of the 1861-65 Civil War: 'Nothing crumbled, no
[on]e deserted; all had to be overpowered, man by man, yard by yard.'
[I] wanted to meet these Southerners who had taken our name for their
[ci]ty. How could I fail to be interested in Birmingham, Alabama?

Alabama is bigger than England, 12,000 square miles bigger.
[A]labama's population is under four million, one million of which is in
[Jo]nes Valley in the Midlands.

Jones Valley is seven miles wide, 70 miles long and 600 feet above sea
[le]vel. In April, when I was there, the temperature was in the eighties.
[Bi]rmingham rests in the valley. About 100 years ago, or a little earlier,
[th]ere were deer and bears. It is still a semi-paradise.

From the ridge of the valley you can see the whole of Birmingham.
[T]here are some fine buildings. The population is above 300,000.
[Bi]rmingham links with nearby towns and suburbs making a
[co]nurbation of almost a million souls. Trees camouflage the sprawl.

As an English visitor, goodwill towards me abounded. After a few days
[fri]ends sprang up like mushrooms. Food, motel accommodation and
[se]rvices were excellent. Television and radio less so; be smart, save money
[w]as the all too-frequent advertising theme.

Birmingham, Alabama – planned in 1871 before motor-cars were
[th]ought of – owes its existence to four factors: minerals, war, railways and
[pr]ivate enterprise.

In the 1840s iron ore, and later coal and limestone were found in
[Jo]nes Valley. These minerals were adjacent and abundant. By 1860
[ra]ilroads to exploit this wealth had been surveyed. One track was to come
[d]own from Chattanooga in the north; and the other to ascend from
[M]ontgomery in the south. The junction would be in Jones Valley. Here,
[su]rely, must be the site of an industrial city?

In the Deep South slavery was a special institution and provided labour
[fo]r the cotton plantations. Indeed 'slavery had become so necessary that
[it] had ceased to appear evil.' The North thought otherwise.

Civil war broke out in 1861. Railroad plans were pigeon-holed. When
[th]e war ended in 1865, the North was victorious but heavily in debt. The
[So]uth was crushed; but the spirit of independence – a sense of difference
[–] still lingers.

By 1870 the construction of the railroads was resumed. A year later
[th]e junction crossing was pin-pointed and the surrounding area bought by
[a] private corporation, the Elyton Land Company. Plots were advertised
[an]d auctioned.

It is difficult for us in crowded England to imagine a private company
[ac]quiring land to build a city. But the speculation was none the less

*Civil War. The United States in 1861.*

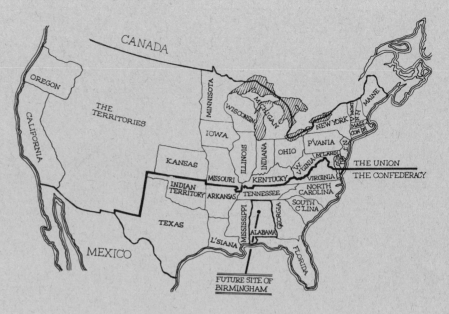

*H886 Arlington Museum, two miles from Birmingham's city centre. This former
plantation mansion was built in 1822 and at the close of the Civil War was the
Union headquarters of General James A. Wilson. From Arlington General Wilson
ordered the burning of Alabama's university and the destruction of the early iron
furnaces in the valley. Concealed in the mansion's attic—so legend says—was the
poetess Mary Gordon Duffee who walked fifteen miles to warn Confederates of the
Union's plans. Seen in the picture are three of the students, in charming period
frocks, who act as Arlington guides. Left to right: Miss Cindy Gibbs,
Miss Teresa Poor and Miss Cindy Coleman.*

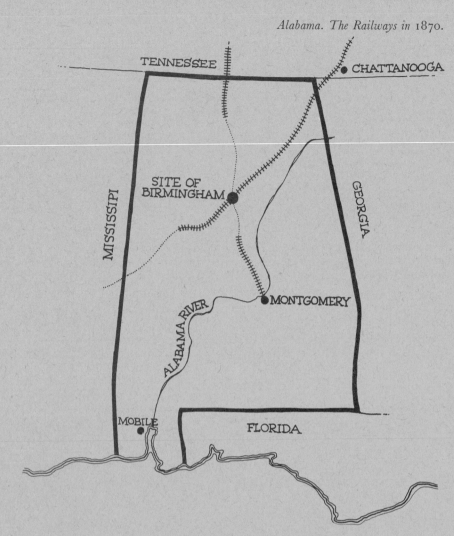

*Alabama. The Railways in 1870.*

TENNESSEE

● CHATTANOOGA

MISSISSIPPI

SITE OF
BIRMINGHAM

GEORGIA

ALABAMA RIVER

● MONTGOMERY

MOBILE
●

FLORIDA

inspired. Spaces were reserved for churches of all kinds, parks were planned, and the streets were to be a hundred feet wide.

There are at least twelve Birminghams. Nine are in the United States, one in Canada, and one (New Birmingham) in Eire. The original is in Warwickshire. The folk in Alabama considered it 'the best workshop in all England' and so took our name for their own. Were there no personal links? I am still trying to discover them.

'The City to be built in the County of Jefferson, State of Alabama, shall be called BIRMINGHAM.' Thus the land company decreed. By 19th December, 1871, the new-born City received its charter. There were then about 1,000 inhabitants, mostly young, mostly ex-servicemen, determined to start life afresh and make their city go.

Forward it sent. In 100 years it has become the industrial and medical capital of the South. In 1969, in comparison with the rest of Alabama, Birmingham was described as 'an island of racial amity in a troubled sea of racial conflict.'

In 1971, Birmingham was named an "All American City" because of racial and cultural progress.

Before my visit to Birmingham, Alabama, I had tried to do some homework. Not much material was available. I met only a discreet silence based on vague memories of distant riots. There was a generous amount of dull interest in my proposed trip.

Alderman Victor Turton, the then Lord Mayor, was different. He gave me encouragement and sent a letter of introduction to his counterpart Mayor George G. Seibels Jr. He was different, too. Back came his welcoming reply. I made my preparations with the help of Mr. T. G. Downe the Lord Mayor's secretary.

I did not go to Birmingham, Alabama, on a civil rights fact-finding tour. And I was only going there for five minutes, so to speak. But naturally I was involved. No man is an island. On the other hand it wasn't my business. I didn't find this contradiction a handicap. Over there they accepted me as I was, warts and all.

As late as 1930, convicts in Alabama were worked in chains. In 1963 there were riots in Birmingham and people were killed at the time when integration was enforced. That was the turning point. Since 1963 the two communities, two-fifths black and the rest white, have lived in almost unbroken peace beneath the shield of a progressive city. More than that, they are working together for a better future. Mutual respect and trust is growing. Certainly that is the official line. Do I believe it? Yes.

I went on no conducted tours. My visit wasn't like that. As a private individual I spoke to anybody I pleased. By chance I talked to a Reserve Deputy Sheriff, a volunteer who pays for his own uniform. He wore a revolver on his hip; a filled cartridge belt carried a torch and a bright pair of handcuffs.

I asked him why he joined. He told me that he had become a part-time policeman because law enforcement is not easy and he wanted to prove to himself that he could do it. He believed in pursuasion. Talking to people was better than shouting at them. Of course it didn't always work. Sometimes advantage was taken of a reasoned approach, but he was convinced it was the lasting way. He had been a Reserve Deputy Sheriff for four years.

I enquired if he had ever used his gun? 'Never. I half-drew it once. It was enough. But I wished I hadn't done even that.'

I spoke to a Negro who, not by choice, had been involved in the 1963 riots. He had suffered grievously. I do not use the word lightly. I asked him if he still felt bitter? 'No,' he said, 'I don't think so. At least I tell yself I'm not. I can't be sure.'

He went on to say how his father had taught him never to be a slave
to prejudice. Since then he had disciplined his mind to be free. Freedom
was what you thought about other people – not what they did to you.

Democracy in Birmingham, Alabama, seems to mean that you can
approach authority direct. I went to the City Hall and asked the clerk at
the inquiry desk if I could speak to the Chief of Police. He picked up the
telephone. 'Is that you, Chief? There's a Mr. John Whybrow here from
Birmingham, England. He wonders if you could spare him a few
minutes? . . . Yes, *Sir*!'

He put the telephone down. 'The Chief will be very pleased to see you,
Mr. Whybrow. Just go right through that door.' It would be misleading
to pretend that earlier arrangements had not been made. They had.
But the receptionist didn't know and no time had been fixed.

I had their annual police report. I handed the Chief a copy of ours.
He called in some of his senior colleagues and they compared identical
breakdowns of two cities 4,500 miles apart. Murder, rape, robbery,
assault, and so on. In 1963 their figures were divided into whites and
coloureds. No longer.

Most of the senior officers, like me, were ex-servicemen between whom
there is often an immediate bond. Nationality seems irrelevant. I asked
any question I liked.

I came from that discussion knowing that keen brains were peering
beyond my vision to protect the spirit of racial co-operation. The problems
to be solved are profound, but I am sure they have the strength to tackle
them. I was reminded of Edward Grey's remark that the United States is
like 'a gigantic boiler. Once the fire is lighted under it there is no limit
to the power it can generate.'

Integration is part of the civic jigsaw puzzle. Birmingham is building a
new civic centre; and accommodating a vast medical campus; and sorting
out pollution; and striving to become 'Greater Birmingham' to increase
the revenue in order to do many more things efficiently. I had time to see
only some of the projects and to meet just a few of the people involved.
Then I had to return home.

At the airport was Mr. Bob Olson, already a friend, the Mayor's
executive secretary. He had come to wish me farewell. He handed me a
packet. The plane took off.

Inside the packet was a three-page letter from Mayor Seibels. He had
been in hospital throughout my visit recovering from a heart attack. We
had exchanged messages through Mr. Olson. But quite apart from those
I had been conscious of his mayoral thrust wherever I went.

From the intensive care unit he had dictated his letter and had included
a batch of reading material. He enclosed, for my wife, a symbolic key to
the city. There was a book for me. On the fly-leaf he had written: "It is a
bitter disappointment not to have had a chat with you and shaken your
hand. Excuse my lengthy letter, but I did want you to get the full picture
of our 'moving' City. My regards to the Lord Mayor and Lady Mayoress.
With every good wish to you – please come back again. Sincerely yours,
George G. Seibels, Jr., Mayor, Birmingham, Alabama."

One day I will return. In the meantime a couple of the friends I made
hope to come here to visit 'the best workshop in all England.' What will
they think of our Birmingham? What's in a name?

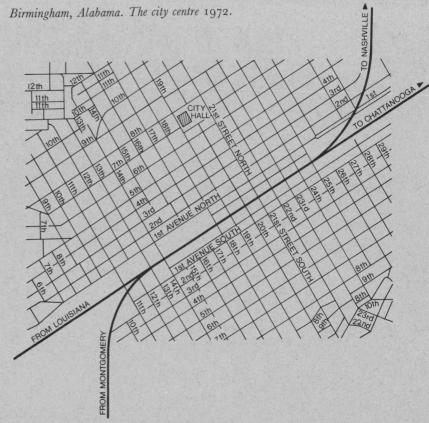

*Birmingham, Alabama. The city centre* 1972.

# Bibliography

## Birmingham: general

The British Association *Birmingham and its Regional Setting. A Scientific Survey* (The British Association, Birmingham Executive Committee, 1950) Re-published, Wakefield, E P Publishers Limited, 1970.

Conrad Gill and Grant Robertson, *A Short History of Birmingham* Birmingham, Birmingham Information Bureau, 1938.

William Hutton *An History of Birmingham* Birmingham, J. Guest, Sixth Edition, 1835.

Various authors *Warwickshire and the Shakespeare Country* Harmondsworth, Penguin Guides, 1960.

Tudor Edwards *Warwickshire* London, Paul Elek Limited, 1950.

The Birmingham Post & Mail Limited *The Birmingham Post Year Book and Who's Who 1971-72* Birmingham, The Birmingham Post & Mail Limited, 1971.

Birmingham Small Arms Company Limited *The March of the Piled Arms* Birmingham, Birmingham Small Arms Company Limited, (pamphlet) 1972.

Edward Chitham *The Black Country* London, Longmans, Green & Company Limited, 1972.

J. K. Dent *Making of Birmingham* Birmingham, J. L. Allday and Simpkin Marshall and Company, 1894.

Pike's New Century Series No. 3 *Birmingham at the Opening of the Twentieth Century* Brighton, W. T. Pike & Company, 9 Grande Parade, 1905.

Conrad Gill and Asa Briggs *History of Birmingham* London, Oxford University Press, 1952.

Vivian Bird *Portrait of Birmingham* London, Robert Hale and Company, 1970.

## Birmingham: buildings and architects

Philip B. Chatwin *The Life of J. A. Chatwin, F.S.A.(Scot) 1830-1907* London, Oxford University Press, 1952.

Nicholas Cooper and Nicholas Taylor *The Nineteenth Century Architecture of Birmingham* London, The Victorian Society, 1965.

Nikolaus Pevsner and Alexandra Wedgwood *The Buildings of England – Warwickshire* Harmondsworth, Penguin Books Limited, 1966.

Douglas Hickman *City Buildings Series – Birmingham* London, Studio Vista Limited, 1970.

Bryan Little *Birmingham Buildings – The Architectural Story of a Midland City*, Newton Abbot, David & Charles (Publishers) Limited, 1971.

## Photography

Albert Boni *Photographic Literature: an International Photographic Guide* New York, Morgan & Morgan, 1966.

Helmut and Alison Gernsheim *The History of Photography* London, Thames and Hudson Limited, 1969.

Robin Campbell and Norbert Lynton *'From Today Painting is Dead': The Beginnings of Photography* London, Arts Council of Great Britain, (exhibition catalogue) 1972.

D. B. Thomas *The Science Museum Photography Collection* London, Her Majesty's Stationery Office, 1969.

J. G. Hammond and Company *Birmingham Faces and Places* Birmingham, J. G. Hammond and Company, volumes I-III, 1889-91.

John Whybrow Limited *The John Whybrow Collection* Birmingham, register of original and copy negatives of Birmingham scenes, and elsewhere, 1857 onwards, manuscript, 1972.

John Whybrow Limited *Negative Registers* Birmingham, list of photographs taken 1911 onwards, manuscript, continuing.

John Whybrow Limited *Contact Two* Birmingham, John Whybrow Limited, pamphlet on New Street, Birmingham, 1895, 1971.

John Whybrow Limited *Minute Book* Birmingham, December 1913 onwards, manuscript, continuing. Also *Purchase Ledger* Birmingham January 1912 – June 1931, manuscript.

Barbara M. D. Smith *The History of John Whybrow Limited* Birmingham, typescript, 1964.

## Birmingham, Alabama

Executive Committee *Portrait of Birmingham, Alabama* Birmingham, Alabama, Birmingham Centennial Corporation, 1971.

Donald A. Brown, Editor *Birmingham* Birmingham Alabama, centennial keepsake issue, magazine, Birmingham Area Chamber of Commerce, 1971.

H. M. Caldwell *History of the Elyton Land Company and Birmingham, Alabama* Birmingham (Elyton Land Company 1892), reprinted by Caldwell-Garber Company, Birmingham, Alabama, 1926.

John C. Henley Junior *This is Birmingham* Birmingham, Alabama, Southern University Press, 1960.

John C. Henley III, Editor *Early Days in Birmingham* Birmingham, Alabama, Southern University Press, 1968.

John Osborne *The Old South* New York, Time-Life Books, Time Incorporated, 1968.

City of Birmingham *Annual Report* 1970 Birmingham Police Department, Birmingham, Alabama, 1971.

## Corrections

It has not been possible in a number of cases to date with certainty the early photographs in this book. Any corrections would be gratefully received as would confirmation of dated photographs. *Editor.*

# Acknowledgements

The old photographs
Thomas Lewis 1844-1913
Henry Joseph Whitlock 1834-1918

The new photographs
Elizabeth Clair Jones b.1946

Preparation for this book followed immediately after the first 'How does your Birmingham grow?' exhibition, held at the offices of The Birmingham Post from 21st February to 18th March, 1972. Included below are those who helped either with the exhibition or the book, and in many instances with both. Their support and advice is most sincerely appreciated.

Alderman F. T. D. Hall, Lord Mayor of Birmingham 1972-3

Alderman Victor E. Turton, Lord Mayor of Birmingham 1971-2

Alderman Stanley Bleyer, Deputy Mayor 1971-2

The Rt. Hon. Peter E. Walker, M.B.E., M.P. Secretary of State for the Environment

Honorable George G. Seibels Jr., Mayor, Birmingham, Alabama

Mr. Robert Olson, Executive Secretary to the Mayor, Birmingham, Alabama

Mr. T. G. Downes, Secretary to the Lord Mayor, Birmingham, England

Mr. D. J. Bowyer, General Manager, Rackhams Harrods Ltd.; Directors of The Birmingham Post & Mail Ltd.; Mr. F. W. Bradnock, Birmingham Information Department; Mr. Maurice Bright, Miss Marilyn Crowther, and Mr. John Goff of The Birmingham Post; Mr. Anthony Gunstone, Birmingham Museum and Art Gallery; Mr. J. C. Harkness, City Architect's Department; Dr. R. J. Hetherington; Mr. D. H. Hopkinson, Editor, The Birmingham Post; Mr. John Hudson, Hudsons Bookshops Ltd.; Mr. L. Livesey and Mr. S. A. Gibson of Sandbrook Metcalf & Co. Ltd.; Miss D. McCulla, Birmingham Reference Library; Mr. J. A. Maudsley, Birmingham City Architect; Mr. C. S. Pick, Managing Director, William Heinemann Ltd.; Mr. James A. Roberts, Architect; Mrs. B. M. D. Smith; Mr. W. A. Taylor, City Librarian; Mr. David H. Whitlock.

I am also indebted to those connected with Birmingham, England who were kind enough to give me introductions to their counterparts in Birmingham, Alabama, or who assisted me in other ways:

Mr. G. E. Baker, Manager, Sparkbrook Branch, Lloyds Bank Ltd.; Mr. I. Bailey, Commandant, Police Training College; Mr. David Barclay, Secretary, West Midlands Region, Royal Institute of British Architects; Mr. and Mrs. Maurice Bulpitt; Mr. K. A. P. Boyes, Vice-President, Institute of Incorporated Photographers; Miss Barbara Crossette, The Birmingham Post; Sgt. C. Elworthy, Police Training College; Mr. Reginald Eyre, M.P.; Mr. Desmond Foster; Mr. John Greenfield; Mr. K. Harvey, General Manager, Salvage Department; Mr. L. Jenkins, Birmingham Chamber of Commerce; Mr. P. D. Knights, Deputy Chief Constable; Mr. R. J. Medlam, Assistant Regional General Manager, Lloyds Bank Ltd.; Miss Eileen McKenna; Councillor J. C. Silk; Professor D. S. Shovelton; Mr. David Wheeler, President, Institute of Incorporated Photographers; Mr. Richard C. Whitehead, Engineer and Manager, Birmingham Water Department.

The following ladies and gentlemen, amongst many others, made me most welcome during my visit to Birmingham, Alabama from 17th to 27th April, 1972, and provided valuable background material. I wish to record my grateful thanks.

Mr. James E. Adams, Architect; Mr. H. Cleytus Broyles, Director of Public Works; Mr. Donald A. Brown, Editor, 'Birmingham', Birmingham Area Chamber of Commerce; Miss Ethel Bush; Mr. R. J. Cefalu; Miss Cindy Coleman; Mr. T. H. Cowden; Rev. J. T. Crutcher, Minister, 16th Street Baptist Church; Mr. Stanley M. Erdreich Jr., Vice-President, The First National Bank of Birmingham; Mr. I. J. Foster; Miss Cindy Gibbs; Mrs. Susan I. Hartsfield; Mr. John C. Henley III, President, Birmingham Publishing Company; Mr. A. C. Keily, Photographer; Mr. Duard LeGrand, Editor, The Birmingham Post-Herald; Mr. Chris McNair, Photographer; Lieut. L. D. Milwee, Birmingham Police Academy; Mr. Arnold H. Moncrief, Superintendant, Streets and Sanitation Department; Mrs. Gladys Morrow; Mr. Graydon L. Newman Jr., Attorney at Law; Capt. J. C. Parsons, Police Department; Miss Teresa Poor; Miss Richardena Ramsey, Director, Birmingham Library; Mr. W. Roberts, Superintendant, Birmingham Water Works; Mr. George Stewart, Deputy Director, Birmingham Library; Mr. Mel Stout; Capt. L. A. Tate, Police Department; Mrs. Alice B. Walker, Birmingham Beautification Board; Mr. Sam Wesson; Mr. J. A. Warren, Chief of Police; Mr. Carl F. Wittichen, Chairman, Birmingham Reality Company.

Contributors

John Broadhurst: born Birmingham 1947. Graphic Designer. Staff designer John Whybrow Limited. Diploma in Design, Birmingham College of Art. Licentiate, Society of Industrial Artists and Designers.

Martin Hedges: born Cheltenham 1932. Journalist. Successively reporter, news editor and features editor of The Birmingham Post. Now freelance writer. Member, National Union of Journalists; Member, Institute of Journalists.

A. Douglas Hickman: born Birmingham 1932. Architect. Author of Birmingham, a gazetteer of the city's buildings. Founder member of the Birmingham Group of the Victorian Society. Practising architect with The John Madin Design Group. Associate, The Royal Institute of British Architects.

Elizabeth Jones: born Rochford, Essex 1946. Photographer. Staff photographer Windsor Studios, Umtali, Southern Rhodesia, Cadbury Schweppes Limited and John Whybrow Limited. Associate, The Royal Photographic Society.

Edwin Martin: born Nottingham 1932. Photographer. Member, Society for Photographic Education. Head of School of Photography, City of Birmingham Polytechnic. Associate, Institute of Incorporated Photographers.

John Whybrow: born Birmingham 1924. Photographer. Council member, Institute of Incorporated Photographers. Chairman John Whybrow Limited. Associate, Institute of Incorporated Photographers.

Finally I would like to thank members of John Whybrow Limited who assisted in so many ways behind the scenes:

John Broadhurst, Mrs. Jennifer Green, Cyril Holmes, Elizabeth Jones, Elizabeth Kench, Gordon Matthews, Jonathan Roe, and Mrs. Doreen Smith.

*John Whybrow, Editor.*

# ndex and Glossary